WRITING FROM EXPERIENCE

A STEP-BY-STEP GUIDE TO FREELANCE WRITING

AMANDA WILKINS

SUMMERSDALE

Summersdale Publishers
46 West Street
Chichester
PO19 1RP

A CIP catalogue record for this book
is available from the British Library.

Printed and bound in Great Britain.

ISBN 1 873475 89 6

For Hugh who encouraged me from the beginning

and

Peter who is always there to give me helpful advice.

ACKNOWLEDGMENTS

Thanks go to the following magazines for allowing me to reproduce my articles in this book:

Yours Magazine	*The Golden Hinde Sails Again*
	Mr Moonlight and his Leading Lady
Saga Magazine	*Kathy's Batty About Nora*
	From Bernardo to Bronte
	A Legend Holds Court
My Weekly	*Oliver's Travels*
	Lynne McGranger - At Home and Away
Theatre Magazine	*Cameron Mackintosh - The Music Man*
The Buzz	*After Hollywood...Eastbourne*
Tennis Post	*Coaxing Cox*

Thanks also to Sussex Express who have encouraged me, trained me and supported me over the years.

Finally, thanks to Ed Douglas of BBC *Southern Counties Radio*, the Presenter of *The Late Show* who nurtured me from the beginning of my broadcasting career, and always put me at my ease.

CONTENTS

Foreword....7
Fact or Fiction - What is the difference?....9
In The Beginning....13
Types of Article....18
The Golden Hinde Sails Again....19
That Book: One is Not Amused....24
Kathy's Batty about Nora - Interview with Kathy Staff....31
Oliver's Travels - Interview with Tom Oliver....34
It's a Dog's Life....36
Profile of Courage - Kimberly Dell....38
Types of Market....42
We All Make Mistakes....46
How Will I Survive?....49
Specialisations....50
Broadcasting....55

Appendix A - Celebrity Interviews
Exclusive Interview with H.R.H. the Duke of Edinburgh....58
Mr Moonlight and his Leading Lady - Frankie Vaughan....61
After Hollywood...Eastbourne - Michael Praed....64
Profile - Sir Cameron Mackintosh....67
From Bernardo to Bronte - George Chakiris....70
A Legend Holds Court - Ken Rosewall, Exclusive....74
At Home And Away - Lynne McGranger....78
Coaxing Cox - Mark Cox....82

Appendix B - Useful Addresses
Organisations....85
Publications....89

FOREWORD

When I started writing seriously I read every book that was available on the subject. They were all written by 'experts in their field' who had made their name and were now passing on tips to their would-be successors.

They were packed with very valuable information, and I devoured each and every page, but at the end I still felt there was something missing.

What I wanted was an autobiographical book about how they got started; where they made their mistakes and how they suffered what I was suffering, the pangs of rejection and the long periods of despair when you wonder if anything you write is ever going to be published.

They cannot all have started out rich and famous and yet, apart from their biography on the back of the book, there was nothing about their personal feelings as they struggled to succeed. Did they ever wonder if they were going to make it?

I am neither rich nor famous, but after several years of struggling I am beginning to succeed. I can now telephone an editor and get straight through, or fax an idea for a feature and get a reply almost by return - yes, go ahead, or no, not for us this time.

As the pile of magazines containing my published work continues to grow, so am I being asked to be 'Guest Speaker' at Writers Groups, and run Workshops at local colleges. The icing on the cake really came when Fred Olsen Cruises invited me to be a Guest Lecturer on their new liner Black Watch cruising to New England in the autumn of 1997.

If I can help some struggling writer on the road to success by this book, then I will have achieved my aim. The least I can achieve by it is to make sure they do not give up.

Rosemary Horstmann writes in her excellent book *Writing For Radio*,

'The most valuable quality any writer can have in breaking into a new market is persistence. If at first you don't succeed try, try again - and again. Persistence and staying power will win through in the end.'

These words are the truest that have ever been written. I know, I have been there.

Many times when I first started I thought about giving up, but each time I re-read this paragraph and decided to stay the course and now I am very glad I did.

Writing has brought me much more than financial rewards: it has brought me friendship that will last the rest of my life. I have discovered stories that moved me to tears, and seen shows that made me laugh so much I could hardly contain myself.

I have met people who were once just faces on the silver screen, and discovered that underneath their glamour they are genuine, caring people.

This is something anyone can do, be they eighteen or eighty, and if my book helps you on your way, I will have succeeded in what I set out to do. Good Luck!

AMANDA WILKINS.
October 1996.

FACT OR FICTION - What Is The Difference?

Fiction is produced entirely from the writer's imagination. It provides readers with escapism and entertainment and although real place names can be used, the characters must bear no relation to any person living or dead otherwise the author could end up as the subject of a very costly libel suit.

Even if a character is based on a person the author knows, that character must not be so thinly disguised as to be instantly recognisable by that person or his or her friends.

Fact can be anything from a news report to a feature submitted to a magazine or newspaper. Like fiction, unless it is a straight news report of some disaster or crime of violence, it should also entertain readers as well as informing them and illuminating a subject.

Fiction is a completely different form of writing to fact, and many successful journalists find it impossible to write fiction because sentences in factual articles must be short and snappy, whereas in fiction they need to be expanded and are often written in a more flowery language.

Once you have decided you would like to concentrate on non-fiction, then you must make up your mind what you want to do. Do you want to make a career of writing, or just write occasional articles in the hope of selling them to the local paper, or, if you are lucky, a national magazine?

There are literally thousands of magazines and newspapers all over the world and there should be enough work for everyone, but sadly it does not work that way. I will touch on markets later on, but first let us look at the two most common types of journalists. These are the **Staff Journalist** and the **Freelance Journalist.**

The bad news is that very few people, myself included who changed careers at a mature stage in my life, have any chance of obtaining a job on a newspaper or magazine as a Staff Journalist unless they have gone through the stringent National Council for the Training of Journalists Pre-Entry course covering all aspects of journalism.

Even local newspapers, which used to be the training ground for would-be reporters, are reluctant to consider anyone who is not fully trained. This is because with rising costs and lowering budgets their staff reporters are pared to a minimum, and they must be able to cover anything from the Local Council Meeting to a complex case at the Magistrates Court.

The laws concerning Local Government reportage are so stringent these days that editors are not prepared to take the risk of employing someone who has not been fully trained in the laws of Libel and Court Procedure.

I heard of one newspaper who was heavily fined because one of their inexperienced reporters wrote that a Defendant was "wearing a dark blue suit". That was considered a personal affront to the Defendant as you are only allowed to report the facts and not make any personal references to the case or any person involved in it.

The good news is that practically anyone who has a flair for writing, the guts and determination to carry on through adversity and knock-backs, and the ability to live on a shoestring can become a freelance journalist. It is unlikely that you will be able to make enough from writing full time to live on, but if you are willing to take part time jobs to supplement your income then you can carve out a very rewarding career for yourself.

If you specialise in something, so much the better, as you will soon build up a reputation for being an expert in that particular field and if your specialisation is something unusual, then you are definitely on to a winner.

Once you start selling articles to magazines you will build up a rapport with a particular contact, probably the Features Editor, and you will find it much easier to get through to them with ideas for future articles as you are a 'known writer'. As your name gets known they will approach you with commissions of their own.

Do not think that just because you are not writing full time you are an amateur. If you are serious about your work and are getting paid for it, then you are just as professional as a staff journalist working full time on the local paper.

To become a member of the National Union of Journalists you have to be able to prove to them that the largest percentage of your earnings comes from journalism, and even then they only accept you as a Temporary Member until you are established. You are allowed temporary membership for three years, re-applying on an annual basis when you are required to provide a list of publications where your work has appeared and photocopies of articles/features you have had published.

It took me two years to achieve full membership, but the only advantage to that is I now have my membership renewed automatically and I am entitled to apply for a foreign Press Card in case I wish to work abroad.

As a temporary member you are still given a Press Card, a very valuable item as it proves you are a bona fide journalist, and you have the backing of the Union behind you.

Perhaps they do not have the power they used to have, but it is well worth joining as writing can be a very lonely profession and there is always someone at the end of a phone to help and advise you. They have helped me more than once since I started on the rocky road to success.

When I got involved with a 'shady' agent (more of that later) they helped me get my material and photographs back from him. When I got a commission out of the blue to photograph a doctor for the Local Health Authority involving no written text they advised me to ask for a fee way beyond my wildest dreams for less than an hour's work. I duly submitted an invoice and they paid up without a word.

I talked about amateurs and professionals and that if you are paid for your work then you are a professional, but there are very strong cases when you should accept assignments for nothing, despite what anyone might tell you.

It might mean you have to take on extra non-writing jobs to supplement your meagre income, but the experience gained from these non-paid jobs is worth far more than money and all the time you are building up a reputation and making valuable contacts.

When I was first approached by the *Sussex Express* to become the Theatre Critic for Eastbourne Theatres they made it clear from the start there would be no pay, but I would get press tickets. I had never reviewed a show in my life and as I love the theatre I jumped at the opportunity. Despite several overtures to the Editor, I am still unpaid, but if I gave up this job I would be the loser.

I get to see every new show in Eastbourne and Brighton, and my theatre criticisms have improved over the years. I get to meet stars like Anthony Newley, George Chakiris and Michael Praed and through these contacts I am able to obtain Celebrity Interviews which do bring in the money.

Through my work for the *Sussex Express* I am now doing a weekly chat show on theatre for BBC *Southern Counties Radio*. Again, this work is unpaid, but when they approached me I grabbed the chance as I have done very little broadcasting.

One of my close friends is a top sports reporter for the BBC and I know he started his career by working for a year for them unpaid.

You should not be ashamed of working for nothing and if established journalists try to tell you otherwise ignore them. The experience is being stored up in the bank to be withdrawn at a later date, and it makes you no less of a person than the highly paid broadcaster or correspondent you hear or read about every day.

So now you are ready to begin on the long, hard road to success, but where do you start?

IN THE BEGINNING

To become a successful writer of any kind, fact or fiction, you must have the inborn desire to write, even if it does not materialise until maturity.

I honestly believe this, because without this inborn desire you won't have the incentive to carry on through the darkest hours when all you get is rejection, or worse still, no replies at all. You wonder where the next penny is coming from, or how you are going to afford the price of a new ribbon for your typewriter, let alone the cost of the food you need to sustain you.

I have written all my life. I used to rush home from school in Derbyshire and sit down at the dining table, bashing out scripts of terrible plays that I sent off with great confidence to Nottingham Playhouse - one of the top theatres in the country.

I could not understand why I never got a reply, let alone why they weren't immediately putting my play into production. Such is the arrogance of youth.

My mother tells me when I was about ten I sold a fashion article to the *Daily Mirror* but I don't remember it and I am sure it was never published.

On leaving school I went to see the Editor of the *Derby Evening Telegraph* and asked for a job. Instead of sending me away with a flea in my ear, he told me to go and interview my father, a Deputy Lieutenant of the County. He refused to be interviewed and my journalistic career came to a standstill before it had even begun.

In those days I was not really serious about this course of career, and it is my greatest regret now that I missed that opportunity.

Another opportunity I missed was when the soap *Compact* was on the television.

Carried away by the glamour of life on a woman's magazine as portrayed by the BBC I wrote to a national magazine. I cannot even remember which one now but surprisingly I was invited for an interview. I never went as I was more in love with *Compact*'s Editor Ian Harman, than I was enamoured with the idea of a career on a real magazine: how we rue in maturity the silly mistakes we make in adolescence. The moral of this story is - never let an opportunity pass you by.

What started me on a serious writing career was taking over as Editor of Sussex Lawn Tennis Association's free magazine *Tennis Review*. I had been Publicity Officer for a number of years and I put myself forward when the previous editor announced his retirement. He was an expert on all the rudiments of the technicalities of tennis equipment and wrote long and informative articles on these subjects.

I changed the format to include articles, mostly written by myself, and how I enjoyed it. Someone actually said 'At least the editor cannot turn you down'.

Then I saw the advertisement that really changed my life. In one of the Sunday papers I saw the International Correspondence School's advertisement for their courses and one of them was for a Diploma in Freelance Journalism. Immediately I sent for a brochure and was impressed by their syllabus.

I did make enquiries about NUJ accredited courses when they told me they did not recognise the ICS course as a journalistic qualification, but the cost was way above the correspondence or 'distance learning' course the ICS was offering.

Despite not recognising the qualification, the NUJ said by doing the course it showed I was keen and it would do me no harm at all.

You are allocated a Personal Tutor who grades each assignment and sends very useful comments when he returns your work. I found I had to write features I had never even thought of before.

There were assignments on writing for environmental magazines, religious magazines, mass markets, and as the course progressed they got more challenging.

I found it extremely rewarding and when I received my diploma I had it framed with pride. I also sent one of my assignments to the Editor of the *Sussex Express* and he published it. This gave me the entree to the paper which has given me so much help and support over the years.

At the same time as doing the Correspondence Course I attended weekend courses at the lovely Earnley Concourse near Selsey in West Sussex. Run by a very experienced journalist

Hugh Graham these courses *So You Think You Can Write* and *How To Sell What You Write* are hard work but great fun.

Arriving on a Friday afternoon you start work that evening and work through to tea time on Sunday, but there is no pressure because everyone on the course is there with one goal in mind: they want to write. The interchange of ideas between your fellow students and Hugh is very worthwhile and he is an encouraging and sympathetic tutor who takes a genuine interest in his students long after the course is over.

I have repeated these courses more than once and each time I come home stimulated after a great weekend in a beautiful environment. The food is first class and when you do have some leisure time, usually before breakfast, there is an indoor swimming pool which is never overcrowded.

A lot of books say all you need to write is a pencil and paper; there is no need for a lot of fancy equipment. That is quite true, but you will need a decent word processor or computer, especially if you are just beginning.

Editors get hundreds of unsolicited manuscripts every week from would-be journalists, which are opened by one of their underlings and probably read before it even reaches the editorial staff. A badly presented manuscript will be rejected straight away, and an untyped submission will be sent back unread.

Good presentation will not guarantee acceptance but it will certainly be noted and have more chance of being passed on to the right person.

I started off with a basic electric typewriter that did not take anything on disc. The result was a huge photocopying bill, and the necessity to re-type every page I wanted to edit.

When I had my first good sale I bought my first word processor and was able to save everything on disc. It also had a word count so I no longer had the laborious task of counting every page.

Where I made my mistake was my discs were not DOS compatible and when I sold an article to *Commercial Motor* and they asked for it on disc I was in trouble.

Luckily I belong to a tennis club who took pity on me and let me retype it on disc and my article was accepted. Had I not been able to supply it on disc it would have been rejected, and this is becoming the norm with magazines these days.

I invested in my first ever computer and I felt I was in heaven, but when the printer broke down and I was told it would take a month to mend I was completely stuck.

Having sold my word processor to pay for the computer I was unable to meet deadlines and I could see my slowly building career collapsing around me.

Luckily the computer was still under guarantee and by failing to repair it in the stipulated period they had failed to meet the terms of the guarantee. Therefore I had the option of returning it and getting a replacement or cancelling the contract.

Never being computer literate I decided to give it up altogether, and I now work on a Fontwriter Personal Word Processor. The size of a laptop computer, this has all the functions I need. It has a spellcheck and word count, and the discs can be saved as DOS compatible. It has a built in printer and is at a price most struggling writers can afford.

Having got your word processor sorted out, what else do you need? A pocket tape recorder is an essential piece of equipment. Even if you have an A1 shorthand, there is always a danger of your interviewee turning round and saying you have misquoted them. If you have a record of your conversation there is no danger of this happening, but do tell them you are recording the conversation. I have never had anyone object and in fact many of them told me they wished more people used tape recorders.

A notebook and pen goes without saying, but something a lot of writers may not think of is a camera. The chances of selling a feature to a magazine are greatly enhanced if you can supply the photographs as well. Some magazines, like SAGA, always insist on sending their own photographer, but this is an expensive exercise especially if they are based in London, and if you can take a good photograph to illustrate your article your finances will increase.

A good 35mm compact is suitable to start with - I began with a Canon Sureshot with a zoom lens, but if you can afford an SLR camera with interchangeable lenses you will take a better photograph.

I use a Canon EOS 1000 with a 35mm - 70mm lens and I bought a 70 - 210mm lens second hand.

Magazines prefer 35mm colour transparencies because they reproduce better, although some of them will accept colour prints. As you get to know the contacts it is best to ask about illustrations when you put the idea to them and to find out what they require. Newspapers prefer to have black and white prints, although nowadays they can reproduce from colour.

Even though your wordprocessor has a spellcheck, it is always useful to have a good dictionary and an encyclopaedia to hand, plus a world atlas. If you are interviewing an Australian soap star it is less embarrassing to look up their hometown in an atlas when you get home than to ask them how to spell it at the time of the interview.

It is not necessary to set up an elaborate 'office' in your home. A desk in the corner of the sitting room, with a filing cabinet and a set of bookshelves is all you want, as long as you can work in peace with no distractions from the rest of the family.

Now you have your equipment and you are ready to begin - so what type of article are you going to write - and where do you find your markets?

TYPES OF ARTICLE

Features are best described as factual stories with little news value, but plenty of reader interest. There are really only two types of feature, the **Human Interest**, which is designed to tug at the reader's emotions and stimulate love, hate, fear, grief, etcetera, and the **Informative** article where the object is to satisfy the reader's desire to know more about the subject of the feature.

These types are broken down still further into:

1. **The General Interest Feature** which can be used anytime, anywhere, although this sort of feature is more often found in magazines than newspapers.
2. **The News Feature** which usually appears in newspapers rather than magazines as they are linked to current events which are highly topical.
3. **The Travel Feature.**
4. **Celebrity Interviews.**
5. **The Seasonal or Anniversary Feature** relating to specific events or times of the year.
6. **Profiles,** not necessarily of celebrities. These can be of a local businessman or charity worker, or even someone who has overcome some terrible handicap or debilitating illness.

Taking each feature separately, the **General Interest** article should be written in an entertaining way, but at the same time it should include factual information so that the readers feel they really know as much about the subject as the writer by the time they have finished reading it.

General interest stories fall into the informative category and they take a lot of research, because each fact must be checked and double-checked so you don't impart the wrong information.

A good example of a General Interest feature is one I wrote for *Yours Magazine Autumn Special* in 1995. The replica of Francis Drake's Golden Hinde sailed into Brighton Marina and I went down to take some photographs.

She was so splendid that I immediately wanted to find out more about her and I went on board and introduced myself to the Skipper.

Having found what I felt would make a good story I came home and telephoned the editor of the *Best of British* magazine who immediately commissioned a package of text, colour photographs and transparencies.

She was in Brighton for a month and I went down every day, talking to members of the crew and visiting Musketeers, taking photographs from each and every angle.

I did far more interviews than I needed, and took far too many pictures, but it is much easier to discard unwanted material than it is to pad out a feature because you have not got enough.

I duly submitted my feature and photographs only to receive a telephone call saying they now wished to use it in the *Yours Magazine Autumn Special*, rather than in its smaller stablemate the *Best of British*. The feature and photographs are reproduced below.

THE GOLDEN HINDE SAILS AGAIN

AMANDA WILKINS goes on board and meets the modern-day crew of this beautiful reproduction of a sixteenth century warship. Sir Francis Drake would definitely approve!

In June 1579, a small English ship, the Golden Hinde, beat her way northwards off the west coast of America. Her Commander was Francis Drake, admiral, explorer, and privateer, returning home from his circumnavigation of the world.

The ship was laden with a fortune in treasure seized on the Pacific coast from the surprised Spanish.

Even this 16th century warship had been seized by one of history's most colourful characters.

Originally called the Pelican, Drake changed her name to the Golden Hinde, the old English name for female deer, because it was featured in the Hatton family coat of arms. Christopher Hatton (of Hatton Garden in London fame) was one of the principal sponsors of Drake's world voyage.

In April this year a full-size reconstruction of this famous ship sailed past Brighton's Palace Pier on her way to the marina where she was due to remain for a month before going on to Portsmouth.

The only concession to the 1990s is the fact that she is steered, for safety reasons, by a conventional wheel instead of a whip staff (a pole attached to a rudder) which Drake used, and she had to motor into her berth rather than sail right up to the harbour wall.

Designers spent several years researching to ensure the new ship would be authentically constructed, and traditionally hand-crafted. She was built in Devon, the keel was laid on September 30, 1971, three months after construction began, and she was officially launched in 1973.

After the launch the Golden Hinde sailed to San Francisco where she spent some time as a memorial to Drake's landing in California and claiming it on behalf of Queen Elizabeth I.

She then retraced Drake's route across the Pacific and Indian Ocean to England to complete her own circumnavigation of the world in 1980. She was established as an educational museum in 1981 and berthed in Great Britain until 1984, before sailing to the Caribbean and touring America and Canada.

She is now back in Britain, once again giving schools the opportunity to visit her so the pupils can see for themselves the sort of conditions Elizabethan sailors had to put up with.

Each weekend the ship entertains visitors with all the crew dressed in period costume, taking you back to the Elizabethan period. It is not unusual to hear the sound of musket fire echoing over the harbour wall!

I met Saul, who dresses in period costume and plays the part of a sailor who sailed with Captain Drake and was with him when he travelled round the globe.

He thrilled his audience, mostly children, with his tales of the trip and how the best part for him was the Straits of Magellen.

The first captain of the new Golden Hinde was Adrian Small and he remained with the ship until 1979. Now the Operations Manager in charge of her at each port of call is Captain Philip Smith who joined the crew in March.

He is joined on each voyage by the Director of Golden Hinde Ltd, Roddie Colman.

The crew are very cosmopolitan and many of them have had little or no sailing experience when they join the ship. They are trained not only in seamanship, but also as tour guides and they dress in Elizabethan costume every day to show parties around the ship.

The costumes are made by a seamstress and kept in a store and handed out to new crew members when they arrive.

In port the crew sleep in bunks in Portacabins near the ship, but at sea they sleep in hammocks on the gun deck where the ceiling is so low you can't stand up straight.

This is another concession to the present day as in Drake's day they would have had straw pallets on the wooden deck!

Senior crew member is Christopher Saunders, who has been with the Golden Hinde for just over a year. Chris graduated from Newcastle with a degree in ancient history and he was thrilled to have found this job.

"I wanted to find a job connected with history and there aren't many of those around," he told me. "To find a reconstruction of a 16th century sailing ship is absolutely brilliant."

Chris's sailing experience only stretched as far as one week's sailing in Australia before he joined the Golden Hinde, but he has picked it up over the past year and is now watch leader when they are at sea. He also trains the new crew members in seamanship and as tour guides.

Photo: Amanda Wilkins

I met two very new recruits in Brighton. Lincoln Manuel and Trisha Sullivan had only been with the ship for two days when I spoke to them. New Yorker Lincoln had flown from America especially to join the Golden Hinde.

"I have a very good friend in New York who spent one and a half years on her," he said. "I was won over by her stories and felt I must join the ship."

You can stay on the Golden Hinde as long as you want to, and as long as you are happy with the job, and Lincoln has committed himself until September when he has to return to America to study.

Twenty six year old Trisha Sullivan comes from Minnesota. She arrived in England for a working holiday and heard about the Golden Hinde from the organisation who supplied her work permit. She is using her experience on the ship as a bridge between acting, which she did when she was younger, and education which she is going into.

"I am signed on until the end of July," she said, "then I have to go back to the University of Minnesota to do my education degree."

She told me she was really looking forward to her first voyage although it was going to be very different. "I have only sailed 26-footers on little lakes before," she said.

The only Canadian aboard is twenty four year old Lisa Strong who is the cook. When I met her she was preparing the food for the voyage to Portsmouth.

"It's quite a task as we have 27 on board," she said. "That's twice as many as usual, but the re-enactors and the musketeers are coming with us this time."

Lisa graduated with a communications degree 18 months ago and decided to travel for two years. She was working in a French ski resort before she joined the ship. She leaves when the ship gets to Portsmouth to go to Egypt, Turkey and Israel.

"I was a bit apprehensive before I joined," she said, "but the crew are marvellous and that's what makes the ship. It's definitely been a great experience and I can highly recommend it to anyone who wants to see England but doesn't want to stay in London. You meet people of every nationality and you get to see the country. You are also in a position where people come up to talk to you, you don't have to make the first move."

I was sad when the Golden Hinde sailed out of Brighton. I had visited her virtually every day for the month she was there and had got to know the crew, and I could see why Lisa was so enthusiastic about them.

I could also quite easily imagine what it must have been like to sail on the Golden Hinde in Drake's time.

This is one of the most perfect reproductions of a 16th century vessel and like the original, there is no heating and no running water. It is living history at its best.

Photo: Amanda Wilkins

THE GOLDEN HINDE FACTS AND FIGURES

BUILT BY - J Hinks and Son, Appledore, Devon, England.
LAUNCHED - April 5, 1973
LENGTH - Overall 120 ft, Hull 102 ft, Waterline 75 ft, Beam 20 ft.
HEIGHT Mainmast 92 ft.
SAIL AREA 4,150 sq. ft.
DISPLACEMENT 300 tons
SAILING SPEED 6-8 knots, 7-9 m.p.h.
GUNS - 2 Peteras (small guns) on poop deck,
2 Peteras on fo'c'sle deck,
2 Falcons (long range guns using two pound shot(in fo'c'sle,
14 Minions (guns using four pound shot) on gun deck.
LATIN MOTTO (on back of ship) Cassis Tutis Sima Virtus
(Virtue is the Safest Helmet) comes from Christopher
Hatton's Coat of Arms.

Published in Yours Magazine, Autumn Special. October 1995

News Features are more difficult than General Interest Features, because they relate directly to events currently in the public eye. These features must not be confused with the reports of these events, mostly covered by staff journalists.

Features can include the writer's own opinions, whereas reports must stick strictly to the facts, but both the report and the feature must be of current interest to the reader.

I rarely write News Features as you have to be in the right place at the right time, but I did write one for the *Sussex Express* in October 1994 when Anna Pasternak's book *Princess In Love* was hitting the headlines all over the world.

Sussex Express Freelance Writer Amanda Wilkins reports on 'that book' which has fascinated the nation

THAT BOOK: ONE IS NOT AMUSED

Never was such a veil of secrecy drawn over any book. Never was a book on the shelves so quickly after the speculation it had been written.

Front page news in all the Sunday papers, then it was in the shops. No advance publicity about its content. No serialisation in the tabloids.

Princess In Love is the story of a supposed five-year love affair between the Major, who turns out never to have reached that rank, and the wife of the heir to the throne.

The author, Anna Pasternak, said in a television interview she did not write it for the money. She wrote it because she felt James Hewitt's love and support for Diana was so lovely it had to be told. Excuse me whilst I just go and throw up!

Being a struggling writer myself, I decided I had to see it for myself. I convinced myself I must keep up with the news and I was not just interested in scandal. That's my story and I'm sticking to it!

So, was it available in Lewes? I walked into Sussex Stationers and asked: "Have you got this new book?" The assistants pretended they didn't know what I was talking about. "What new book?" they said.

"The one that's been in all the headlines," I told them. "Oh, that." They dismissed it as if the very theme was beneath contempt, which it is of course. "It's only available in London."

I walked down the hill to Unicorn Books, but as I know the owners I lost my nerve about asking them. One look round the shop told me they had not got it anyway, so I continued down the hill, convinced that it was not available locally.

Before I went to collect my car I popped into Cliffe Post Office, which is incorporated with John Menzies. I rounded a corner of the stand - and there it was! Surreptitiously I picked up a copy and sidled up to the counter.

"I'd better have one of these," I said, nonchalantly. "Well, you're not the only one," the girl said. "They've only been out there half an hour and we've nearly sold out. The Manager had to check before they went out if we were allowed to sell them."

My mother, an ardent royalist, asked me how I could buy such scurrilous rubbish. I told her it was an investment and I would sell it after I had read it. Does that make me as bad as the author?

I have not had time to read it yet, but what bits I have seen are quite unbelievable. It is like a Mills and Boon novel ... 'Diana stood up and without saying a word, stretched out her hand and led James to her bedroom.'

It is understandable that the ex-Cavalry Officer has been branded a cad by his former friends.

Perhaps, by buying it, I am as guilty as the people who contributed to the book. But, as I was told in John Menzies, I was not the only one and if I had remained in blissful ignorance of its content, it would have made absolutely no difference to the fact it had been published.

Published in Sussex Express October 7 1994.

Travel Articles are extremely difficult to get accepted, simply because there are so many people who want to become travel writers. Most of the national papers have their own Travel Editors and Travel Writers and are unwilling to accept articles from freelances.

There are openings in magazines like *The Lady* for well researched articles on British and Foreign travel, but an unknown writer is unlikely to get a commission so you have to have the money to travel before you sell the piece. Travel companies do give established writers free trips in order to publicise their holidays, but they are not likely to hand out 'freebies' to freelance journalists who do not have a definite commission so it is a vicious circle and a very difficult market to get into. If you do succeed in becoming a travel writer the rewards are very high but it is not the route a beginner should venture down.

I collect hippos. I have a wide selection of all sorts of shapes and sizes in a vast range of materials from bronze to glass. I had an idea that it would make a good feature if I went to find a real live hippo and I wrote to several travel companies.

One very well known company which does high-class safaris took up the idea and offered me a free trip provided I got a commission, and they mentioned a selection of magazines they would like to see the feature appear in.

I was very excited that at last I would achieve my lifelong ambition and travel to Africa but, alas, the magazines were just not interested.

I am fortunate to have received an invitation from Fred Olsen Cruises to travel on their new liner Black Watch to New England in the fall of 1997. I shall be running writing workshops on board, but I am also hoping to write an illustrated feature as the ports of call are steeped in history.

Most travel magazines want more than your own personal opinion of a place, they are not really interested in your views. What they want are facts right down to the price of a cup of coffee and how many lavatories there are in a certain town, are they accessible and do you have to pay to use them?

Although travel features on exotic places make escapist reading, there are also serious travellers due to visit that particular venue who want to know about the place before they go there. They will be making up their own minds so they are not interested in the writer's opinions, what they want are the hard facts.

Celebrity interviews are my forte, they are what I have chosen to specialise in and I thoroughly enjoy doing them. I do them mostly for magazines who want a true picture of their lives away from the stage or screen, and personally I would never work for the tabloids who want to dig up the 'sleaze' rather than ask for a straightforward interview.

Most people in the public eye are very approachable and are very happy to do an interview. In all the years I have been doing them I have only had two refusals, one from a well known television actor who was on tour in a play with his wife. I wrote to him well before they arrived at the Devonshire Park Theatre in Eastbourne inviting them to tea at the town's famous Grand Hotel so that I could talk to them in a relaxed atmosphere. I told them not to bother to reply if it was convenient and I would confirm the appointment when they arrived in Sussex.

I duly left a card at the stage door on the first night informing them I was looking forward to meeting them, but when I went round afterwards I received my own card back with 'Appointment cancelled' scrawled on it and no explanation, but luckily such rudeness is rare.

The other refusal I had was from Anthony Newley, and it was entirely my fault. I was still "green" and I got very excited when *Hello* magazine told me they would accept an interview if I could get him to talk about Joan Collins. I wrote to him on tour in *Scrooge* and told him this and he sent me the most delightful refusal I have ever had, thanking me for my invitation to interview him but regretted he must decline the offer as he was too tired. I did get to meet him at the Press Call and he is a most charming man.

I have turned down the chance to do an interview only once. I had a commission from *My Weekly* to talk to four Australian soap stars in three separate interviews whilst they were over here in pantomime. Two of them readily agreed and I did the interviews, but the other two, a married couple, refused to do it unless I paid them a hefty fee so I politely declined and said 'thanks, but no thanks'.

Unless the magazine is prepared to pay an 'interview fee' to the interviewee, you should never pay out of your own pocket because you will be the loser both financially and, in the long run, it may well jeopardise future interviews. If word gets round the business you are prepared to 'buy' them you may well never get another 'free' interview.

Celebrities will say when asked whether they charge a fee, and it is entirely up to you whether you decide to do it. If it is a previously unobtainable name then the magazine may well be willing to cover the price they are asking in addition to your fee.

Having said that, you should, where necessary, offer hospitality to your interviewee as a matter of courtesy. When I talked to Lynne McGranger (Irene from *Home and Away*) we did the interview in a small café opposite the theatre as we had brunch, and I automatically insisted on paying as she had granted me the interview. She was reluctant to accept at first and she has remained a good friend and writes me lovely letters from Australia.

You can find yourself in amusing situations when doing these interviews as I did when I talked to a British soap star. I had made an appointment with him and duly met him at the stage door after the matinée.

He told me his wallet was locked up in the theatre and he was 'absolutely starving'. I suggested going to the pub next door to get a bar snack but he said he must have a full meal. I ended up paying for both of us, and then never sold the interview.

I know from my fellow students at Earnley that people are afraid of approaching celebrities but they are only human and if you write a frank, honest letter you may be surprised at the response.

My first Celebrity Interview was with Kathy Staff (Nora Batty in *Last of the Summer Wine*). She was appearing in pantomime in Eastbourne and I wrote to her at the theatre explaining I was a 'rookie' journalist and would like to talk to her. I told her I had no commission, and in fact had never done a celebrity interview before. Her husband, who deals with her correspondence, replied with an appointment and Kathy quickly put me at my ease. I tape recorded the interview and made a few notes, then transcribed it when I got home later.

Because she had been so helpful I did a good interview and it turned out to be my first big sale. *Saga* magazine took it and the thrill of seeing your name in print for the first time is a very rewarding experience.

Pantomimes are a very good time to do celebrity interviews. Nearly all of them have a famous name in the cast, and after they have opened they are usually set for a long run so the stars have plenty of time. It may be necessary to arrange the interview through the publicity department, or you can write to the interviewee direct, care of the theatre.

If you have not got a commission, do not tell them you have as it could lead to problems afterwards.

If you have a magazine in mind say you are going to submit the interview, but do not give the impression it will definitely appear otherwise you may get a strong letter from their publicity agent afterwards and your name may well be blacklisted in the business.

Publicity agents are there to protect their clients' interests and you may well find you have a list of instructions prior to the interview, but don't let this put you off the person you are going to see. When I spoke to Tom Oliver (Lou Carpenter from *Neighbours*) I was told he would not do it until I had a copy of his four-page biography. With Michael Praed I was informed he would not allow photographs and we were all allocated our own individual time slot and we must abide by that. Both these actors turned out to be the most unassuming people I have ever met.

When I wrote to Frankie Vaughan he got the Theatre Manager to telephone me with an appointment and when I arrived I was told "You can have fifteen minutes, Mr Vaughan is very tired". Mr Vaughan was not prepared to abide by this time limit and he and his charming wife Stella entertained me to tea in his dressing room and talked to me for well over half an hour. After the interview he wrote to me and told me I was a 'delightful lady' and he was very pleased to know me.

Many women's magazines are reluctant to take on unknown writers for celebrity interviews as they are afraid they might write something libellous, but if you are totally honest and tape record each and every interview, you cannot go wrong.

Use your judgement about your questions and don't make them too personal.

One new magazine, which never made the bookstalls, commissioned me to talk to Nichola McAuliffe (from television's *Surgical Spirit*) when she was appearing at Chichester Festival

Theatre. I arranged this through the Press Officer and she gave me a very good interview.

The lady Editor was not satisfied. "It's all about acting," she said. "I want to know whether she comes from a one-parent family" (almost was she beaten by her father). I felt this was an intrusion of privacy and told Nichola so, and we turned down the interview and Nichola and I have remained on good terms. Two years on I have just sold the interview to a county magazine where she is appearing in pantomime.

One very important rule is never offer magazines interviews you cannot possibly get. An unknown writer is very unlikely to be able to gain access to an American film star filming in England. Even if he or she were willing to grant an interview, you will never get near enough to ask.

Stick to television stars touring the country, or big names appearing in summer shows and pantomime.

The other thing to do if you are approaching a star is to get in touch with the publicity department at the theatre. They will be very helpful and provide you with publicity photographs if you cannot take your own. It is their job to arrange the press calls and they will not be best pleased to find one of their appointments disrupted by an interview completely unknown to them.

You have got your interview, so how do you prepare? First, go to the library and read up everything you can about the star you are going to meet. Telephone the publicity department of the management for the show they are appearing in and ask them to send you a biography.

Once you have the information you can start preparing your interview. It is unlikely you will be allowed much time, so write down each question you want to ask then all you have to do is read out your list and tape their replies.

Celebrity interviews pay well, and you will be the envy of your friends when they read you have met their favourite soap star.

KATHY'S BATTY ABOUT NORA.

She's Britain's most unlikely sex symbol but she's not complaining. By AMANDA WILKINS

She is Britain's most unlikely sex symbol and she is loving every minute of it. Actress Kathy Staff is probably best known to millions of television viewers as Nora Batty, the harridan with the baggy stockings from *Last of the Summer Wine*. Kathy has a soft spot for Nora, she explains: "Playing a lovely character like Nora Batty has opened the door to all the other things such as pantomimes every year. I mean, I can choose the plays and the pantomimes I do, so it's very good being Britain's most unlikely sex symbol. I don't have to worry what I look like!"

Kathy was sitting on the sofa in her dressing room in the Devonshire Park Theatre in Eastbourne where she was appearing in *Dick Whittington*, playing Nora Fitzwarren, complete, of course, with her trademark wrinkled tights and curlers in her hair. In reality she is a very jolly person and it is easy to see why she has captured the heart of Compo and the millions of fans who tune in regularly as clockwork.

She took on the part of Nora Batty when the series started in 1972, and in 1978 she immortalised another popular television character when she became Doris Luke in *Crossroads*. With the two series on TV at the same time, wasn't it rather complicated? "No, not really. They were both completely different characters. I was in *Crossroads* for nine months of the year, then they used to release me for three months to do *Last of the Summer Wine*, so they were completely separate.

"I only had to run straight down from Birmingham to London once, - the very first time. We had arranged a Christmas "Summer Wine". I can't remember if it was a long one or not, when I was asked if I would do *Crossroads.* I rang the producer, Sid Lottersby, who said 'You mustn't miss 18 weeks work (on *Crossroads*) for just one episode. Get the producer to ring me. So I did and they arranged it between them and I did the two in one week, but it only happened once," she explained.

This year Kathy celebrates 45 years in show business. Although she always wanted to be an actress, none of her family had any connection with the stage and her mother felt she should be trained to do something "useful". So she trained as a shorthand typist, after which Kathy's mother told her, "Now you can do what you want," and she went as a drama student to a company in Scotland and started at the bottom.

She served her apprenticeship in the time-honoured fashion with weekly repertory companies throughout the British Isles and it was while she was appearing in Llanelli that she met her husband John. "I was in rep in his home town. I always used to go to church and he was in the choir and used to read the lesson. We met at a New Year's Eve Social they had."

They have been married for 42 years and live in Cheshire where Kathy was born 65 years ago. John deals with all the business letters while she copes with the massive fan mail. Following the birth of two daughters, and prior to "Summer Wine", Kathy did a lot of television work, appearing in four series of *Sez Les* with the late Les Dawson and playing Vera Hopkins of the Corner Shop in *Coronation Street* and Mrs Blewitt in *Open All Hours* with Ronnie Barker.

Her daughters have not followed her into the profession. "Katherine is a dental assistant with the local authority in Cheshire and Susan, the youngest, is a curate with the Church of England. Her church is just outside Chatham so we were able to go there for Christmas Eve Midnight Communion and spend Christmas Day with her," she said.

At an age when most people are thinking of putting up their feet, Kathy sings, dances and takes part in a knife-throwing act in pantomime. How does she keep so fit? "It must be all the work because this year I haven't stopped. I did panto last year with Paul Henry who used to play Benny in *Crossroads*, which meant I could live at home. Then I did manage just over two weeks' holiday before I started in an 18-week tour of *Two Into One*, the Ray Cooney farce. I had three weeks between the end of the tour and *Sailor Beware*, but that's when we filmed "Summer Wine".

Later I had to travel from Norwich to London then from Cardiff to London for studio work on the series. I finished the tour on the Saturday then started pantomime on the Monday."

So what does the future hold for the busy Mrs Staff? "I have no firm plans at the moment. I'm not doing anything for a month, then we're starting another series of "Summer Wine" in the Spring. So I'll be at home in Cheshire for at least two weeks, then we'll probably have a holiday - go somewhere nice and warm."

Kathy would love to do a musical but as *Last of the Summer Wine* looks set to run and run she may not get the chance.

"Last year, after 21 years, the BBC gave us a certificate to say we were the longest running comedy series in the world; last week I read in *The Stage* it is still the top comedy show. So they're not going to let it go.

"I think as long as the men agree to do it, I say the men because they are so much older than we are. Bill (Owen) is 80 this year, but Roy Clark says as long as the BBC want it, he will continue to write it."

Yes, but will Compo get his wicked way with Nora Batty? Kathy isn't saying but she does say that maybe it would spoil the show if he does.

Published in SAGA Magazine March 1994.

OLIVER'S TRAVELS

As a young lad from Hampshire, popular *Neighbours'* star Tom Oliver was all set for a life on the ocean wave, until he dropped anchor in the wonderful land of Oz...

To fans of Neighbours, Lou Carpenter is a stalwart citizen, Mayor of Erinsborough and fair-dealing owner of Carpenter's Cars.

Although little is known of Lou before his arrival in Ramsey Street, the same can't be said for actor Tom Oliver who plays him. His early life reads like something out of *Boys' Own*.

Born in Chandler's Ford in Hampshire, he moved with his family to Fareham when he was two. As he grew up, he desperately wanted to become a jockey, as the Oliver family have been connected with horses for over 200 years.

"I went for an apprenticeship at fourteen," Tom told me "but I was already nine stone two and still growing, so they told me to forget it."

His second love was the sea, so at 16 he enlisted in the Merchant Navy and joined a tramp steamer as a galley boy, sailing round the Mediterranean.

"I had to peel seven bucketfuls of potatoes a day! I soon got fed up of that and signed up as a steward on a ship sailing between the UK and South Africa, before embarking on round-the world trips."

In 1956 Tom decided to jump ship in Sydney, which seemed as good a place as any to settle down.

"I had just two shillings and ten pence in my pocket - it was a silly thing to do," he admits.

"I got a job in a pub, which I shouldn't have because I was under eighteen. Then one evening the police arrested me - the shipping company had charged me with jumping ship," Tom explains.

"However the court dismissed the case and I was given permission tc stay for six months. I had to report to immigration every week, and if the shipping company had said they wanted me for a job, I'd have been obliged to take it. So I took off for Queensland and went six hundred miles into the bush as my theory was 'You've got to find me first!'" he jokes.

"I spent three years as a stockman on a sheep and cattle station, a wonderful life for a boy in his late teens."

Tom worked his passage back to England in 1959 to see his family but he still had itchy feet, so three months later he joined the NAAFI and was posted to Christmas Island, where he worked for a year.

Returning home, he couldn't settle and decided to go back to Australia overland. However, he came down with dysentery in Iran and hepatitis in India and had to be flown back to England.

"It was very frustrating," he admits. "I was desperate to return to Australia, but by 1962 the waiting list was three years. "So I persuaded a friend, an actor and cameraman, to insist that he needed my help with the company he had set up to shoot commercials in Australia - and three weeks later I was on my way!" Tom recalls.

"In the meantime I had written to Albert Finney who was going to film the story of the outlaw Ned Kelly. I told him about my experience as a stockman and offered to be his stunt double.

"I had a very nice letter back, telling me to get in touch with the casting director in Sydney.

"In the end the film was never made, but two months later I was cast as the lead in a half-hour story in the *Adventure Unlimited* series - and I've never stopped since!"

Tom was aware he had to get rid of his English accent, otherwise his career would be very limited. "So I sat down every day with the newspaper and a tape recorder and worked on other accents until I got them right."

He obviously did get them right, because *Neighbours* is his tenth TV series as a regular character.

Tom lives about 20 miles from Melbourne with his American wife Jan, who works as an executive secretary in the suburbs of the city.

He's loved being in *Neighbours* as cast and crew all get on famously, and it gives him the chance to work with his dear friend Anne Haddy, who plays Helen Daniels.

"She took me under her wing when I first settled here and we've worked together on and off ever since".

After a career in Australia spanning 30 years, last December Tom returned to England to appear in his first ever pantomime, *Jack and the Beanstalk*, at Bexhill-on-Sea.

"It was funny having to learn the lines while I was still in Australia being Lou," he admits. "At one stage I thought I might walk on to the *Neighbours* set and say "fee fi fo fum!"

Published in My Weekly, September 28 1996

Seasonal or Anniversary Features appear in magazines or newspapers at certain times of the year. It might be a full page feature on the Titanic which appears on the anniversary of the sinking, or it might be an article on Winter Motoring.

The assignment from my course that was published by the Sussex Express falls into that category as it referred to dogs being given as Christmas presents and it appeared on 10th December.

IT'S A DOG'S LIFE FOR SOME UNWANTED PRESENTS

A Dog is for life...not just Christmas. So say the car stickers produced by the Canine Defence League, but in just a few weeks time many 'chocolate box' puppies will be greeted with squeals of delight on Christmas morning - only to be dumped on motorways, or left tied to lampposts when the novelty has worn off, or when the reality of the cost of keeping a dog hits home.

Marcia Harris is one of the founder members of Pet Rescue, an organisation set up nearly 30 years ago to deal with animals which have been cruelly treated or abandoned in Sussex.

Asked if the problem was worse in the festive season, she said "Many people abandon old dogs towards the end of the year so that they can get a new puppy for Christmas.

"Pet Rescue deals with around 700 dogs a year, and has a small number of foster homes where the animals are looked after before they are found new homes."

The RSPCA at Brighton was asked the same question.

A spokesman said they now no longer house dogs over Christmas and they have done extensive advertising urging people to think twice before buying a puppy. This has alleviated the problem, but generally it is bad throughout the year.

Dogs have been getting a bad press lately due to the number of attacks on children, but in many cases it is the fault of thoughtless or irresponsible owners, rather than the fault of the animals.

In a recent attack in the north of England, two youngsters were allowed to take a large dog for a walk on their own, and it was far too strong for them to control.

To take on a dog is to make a commitment, but once that commitment is made the rewards are plentiful.

Experiments suggest that pet owners are less likely to have heart attacks than those who have no animals.

Doctors researching into the subject have discovered that stroking a dog or cat each day greatly reduces stress and lowers blood pressure.

Many people have been saved from loneliness by having a pet to talk to and there is nothing so rewarding as coming into the house to be greeted by two bright eyes and a wagging tail which say 'welcome home - you are the most important person in my world'.

Marcia Harris says that some of the animals which come to Pet Rescue are the much-loved pets of heartbroken people who simply cannot keep them any more because of a change in their circumstances.

But many more are because people just cannot resist having a cute little puppy for Christmas with no thought for the years ahead.

Photo: Amanda Wilkins

Published in Sussex Express, December 1993

Profiles fall into the human interest category and are completely different to Celebrity Interviews. These are usually told in the words of the star and are about their rise to fame. Profiles need not be about anyone famous, although celebrity profiles do appear when the story of the star is told by the writer as opposed to it being told by the celebrity.

Profiles can be about a local entrepreneur, or someone who has raised thousands of pounds for charity, and the papers are full of profiles when the New Year's Honours List comes out. The 'unsung hero or heroine' who has just been awarded an honour for their stalwart work is an ideal subject for a profile.

They can also be about someone who has overcome some terrible handicap or disability and I make no apologies for reproducing a Profile I did of thirteen year old Kimberley Dell for the Sussex Lawn Tennis Association magazine *Tennis Review*.

It was the most harrowing story I have ever had to tackle, but it was also the most rewarding because Kimberly's courage and high spirits are an inspiration to everyone.

PROFILE OF COURAGE

When you first meet Kimberly Dell she appears to be like any other teenager. Curled up on the sofa of her parents' bungalow she is twiddling with her fringe as all thirteen year olds do. She laughs a lot as she talks to you and you can imagine her jumping up any minute to disco dance to the latest hits. Then you see her wheelchair.

Her story is one of the most horrific, yet one of the most courageous, stories of our time and she is an example to every able-bodied teenager who may be disgruntled with their lot. Until she was eight years old Kimberly was a normal healthy child attending Hampden Park School in Eastbourne and playing with her friends. One day her mother went to collect her from school and they told her Kimberly had not been well. Sheila Dell takes up the story.

"They thought she had been stung," she said, "because she had a mark on her back but it was an old scar and she looked dreadful. When she came towards me she looked terrible and she was crying because she had this pain in her back.

"Kimberly was at the Junior school and her brother Dean was at the infant school so I had to go over the railway line to pick him up and she started screaming in the car. I was in a line of traffic so I couldn't stop. I eventually pulled off the road and she took her skirt off screaming 'my back, my back' and it was burning all over.

"I rushed her round to the doctors hoping there would be a doctor there. It was about 3.30 p.m. and he just said, "Oh she's in for flu, take her home and give her paracetamol." So I kept her off school. That was on Wednesday, and she went back to school on the following Monday. She still had this terrible pain in her back and what we noticed was she couldn't run or anything. I took her back to the doctor a week later and said 'she's still got this back pain' and they took a urine sample thinking it might be a urine infection. That night she started screaming and she was in such a lot of pain she couldn't sleep.

"We went back to the doctors the next day and I said 'look there's something wrong' and they still insisted it was a urine infection and put her on antibiotics.

"I was told to ring the next day for the results and the receptionist told me it was all clear. But she was crying again so I rang back the doctor and told him and he said it wasn't strictly true the sample was clear. There were white blood cells which indicated a virus. He told me to continue over the weekend with the antibiotics and if she wasn't better on the Monday to bring her back again.

"Late Friday night she was in terrible pain again and started vomiting so we got the doctor out and this was the third doctor we had seen. He told her she had a kidney infection and now she was vomiting it would get rid of the muck in her kidneys and the pain would go.

"I was sceptical that a pain she had had for ten days would suddenly vanish, but I accepted it and he left.

"About midnight I noticed she couldn't keep her back straight. She couldn't lie down and was crying with pain. I was crying and in the end her father made me go to bed and he sat up with her. The only way she could sleep was kneeling on the floor with her head in her father's lap.

"In the early hours of the morning when I got up she said she couldn't feel the top of her left leg and it was red hot to touch. We got the doctor out again and eventually it was discovered she had arteriovenus malformation which means malformation of the blood vessels of the spine.

"What actually happened with Kimberly was she had a haemorrhage of the spine, like when people have a stroke which is a haemorrhage of the brain."

After that her illness progressed very quickly and she was soon confined to a wheelchair. For the first two years she was like a caged animal. They lived in a house then and she could not get out, it is only since they have moved to their bungalow on the

Langney Estate in Eastbourne that she has learnt to adapt to her new life.

Kimberly had no interest in sport at all when she was able-bodied and it was her physiotherapist who suggested she should have tennis lessons. "I thought she was mad," Kimberly said. "I'd never heard of people in wheelchairs playing tennis."

Sue Pegler was doing a lot with wheelchair and deaf tennis players at the Ball Park (now the David Lloyd Club) in Eastbourne and Dalene Viljoen who was coaching there at the time rang Kimberly at home and suggested she came down.

"So we went down there and had a chat," Sheila told me, "and we decided to give it a go."

At first Kimberly found it very hard. "I thought 'I'll never master this" she said. "It's exactly the same as ordinary tennis except we are allowed two bounces. I hated it at the beginning and wanted to give it up, but Sue Pegler made me keep on with it.

"They lent me a racket down there at first and I thought I might as well stick at it because it was something to do. Now I can't imagine my life without tennis."

She entered her first tournament in 1992, quite by chance. "The reason why she went into that competition" Sheila said "was we were at Stoke Mandeville sorting out some callipers and we met Bob Dockerill who organises wheelchair tennis. He came up and said there was a small tournament coming up in Swindon so we ought to bring Kimberly to it."

Kimberly has progressed very rapidly with her game and is currently ranked Number 3 in Great Britain and Number 82 in the World Wheelchair Tennis rankings. After playing in the National Wheelchair Tennis Championships in Sheffield at the end of April this year she was 'over the moon' at being selected to represent Great Britain in the World Team Cup at Nottingham Tennis Centre, which is the Davis Cup of Wheelchair Tennis. This attracted entries from 29 countries and was being played on British soil for the first time.

Kimberly remembers clearly receiving the letter telling her of her selection.

"It came about June," she said, "and I read down the names of who it was but the World Cup didn't really come into my mind. Then it went on 'you have been selected to represent Great Britain in the World Team Cup' and I suddenly felt as if I'd just woken up.

"So I went to my Dad and said 'I've been selected for the World Team Cup' and he was quite gobsmacked and he didn't believe it. Then I went into the kitchen and said 'Mum I've got to tell you something, I don't know how I'm going to tell you. It's bad news. I don't know how to put this, but I've been selected for the World Team Cup."

Kimberly's telling of this story sums up her sense of humour. There is no bitterness in her and she enjoys life to the full. She told me modestly she didn't play too badly in Nottingham which must be an understatement as Great Britain came 4th overall (the Men came 6th) which is the best they have ever done.

Kimberly's schedule this year has been hectic, to say the least. Prior to the World Team Cup she had the best win of her life when she went to Paris and won the French Open Wheelchair Tennis Championships. She won the Final in straight sets 6-1/6-3 and is full of praise for her sponsors Rhone-Poulenc Rorer who made it possible for her to go.

She is also sponsored by Sunrise Medical for her smart three-wheeled chair which she plays tennis in and she is hopeful they will provide her with some clothing.

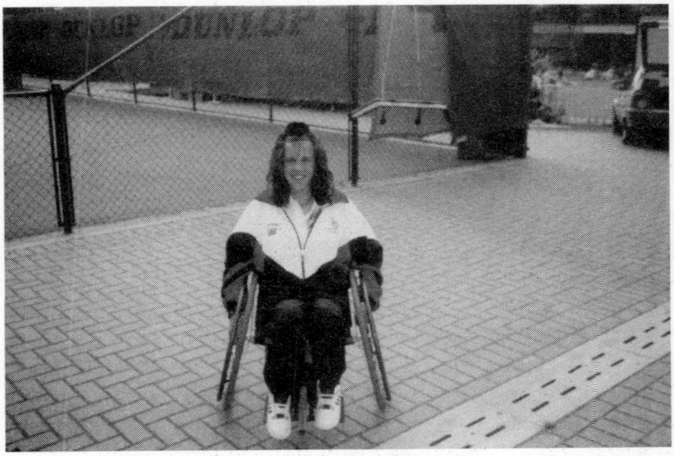

Photo: Sheila Dell

Kimberly has accepted the fact she will never walk again "I can feel one leg, but can't move it," she said, "and I can move the other one but can't feel it and I can't really put weight on either of them."

She is very proud of her trophies which she has displayed on a shelf in her bedroom, underneath which is her pet rat. "He's called Bailey," she said laughing, "after Chris Bailey."

Tennis has definitely changed her life and it would be a tragedy if she had to give this up. There is even a possibility she might be able to go to the Paralympics in Atlanta in 1996. But despite the sponsorship from Rhone-Poulenc Rorer money is the main worry for the Dell family as her father Peter has just been made redundant from his job as a lorry driver, and they just don't know how long they will be able to go on financing Kimberly.

"The cost of Kimberly to go for tennis," her mother said, "is not too high. Once she has paid her entry fee this includes her hotel. But we feel she is too young to travel on her own as she is not fourteen until January 13th 1995 and the cost of Pete to go for six days is £180 bed and breakfast. When Kimberly started she was only eleven and she's still too young to go on her own, so the cost for us is tremendous."

"She was the youngest player ever to be chosen for the World Team Cup" Sheila said proudly.

Kimberly doesn't have any more tournaments until the Nationals at Sheffield in May, then she will think about returning to France to defend her title. In the meantime she works hard at her weekly lessons at the David Lloyd Club with her coach David Gabb. She is the only disabled player at the Club and they are justifiably proud of her success. At a time when British tennis is in the doldrums with no player ranked in the top 100 since the official rankings began in 1975 how good it is to see this lovely, cheerful young lady riding so high in the world of wheelchair tennis.

Published in the Sussex LTA Magazine Tennis Review Winter 1994

TYPES OF MARKET

The first thing that springs to mind when talking about freelance journalism is you must write for magazines or newspapers, but there are other outlets for your work which are a good place to start.

I began by writing for my County Tennis Magazine when I took over as Editor.

Although it was free to members of the Sussex LTA and was not generally available, I still took pride in turning out a good magazine and I still had to meet deadlines, which was very good training in discipline.

If your old school has a magazine, perhaps you could contribute to that, or your local Parish Magazine. Every supermarket now has a magazine and big companies like American Express and Equity and Law have in-house magazines and if you can become a contributor they pay very well.

There are also travel brochures, religious newspapers and advertising agencies who sometimes take work from freelance writers, although as I am 'writing from experience' I cannot really advise on these as I have never written for them.

The best way to contribute to these brochures or agencies is simply to sit down and write to the travel company or agency you have in mind and ask them if they will consider a contribution. But be warned, for this type of feature you must be able to provide a complete package and the photographs must be perfect. Travel brochures want to sell the destinations featured and many of the photographs are taken with filters to make the sky bluer, the beach sandier and if you can produce photographs like that plus a good text you will almost certainly be considered.

Regarding magazines and newspapers, I got a lot of acceptances when I started by contributing to a small monthly publication called *Freelance Market News*.

I also subscribe to *Writers' News* which brings me a glossy magazine once a month and another magazine, *Writing*, four times a year. There is a lot of useful information in these magazines both on fiction and non fictional writing as well as details of competitions anyone can enter.

The 'bible' as far as I am concerned is the *Writer's Handbook* which is published by Macmillan every October. I find it more useful than the *Writers' and Artists' Yearbook* as it contains more information.

The other publication you should refer to (I am not suggesting you purchase it because it is very expensive, unless you can obtain one second hand) is the *Willings Press Guide*. This is published in two volumes, U.K. and Overseas, and contains details of every single magazine and newspaper that is published anywhere in the world.

Reading through these guides you will find that most magazines will not consider 'unsolicited' manuscripts; they prefer you to submit ideas first. Several writing tutors suggest you telephone editors with your idea, but unless you are known to that magazine it is highly unlikely you will be able to break through the barrier of protective staff surrounding him or her.

One very useful tip I learnt from Hugh Graham was to get postcards printed to send in with your idea, and thereafter with your manuscript. If you stamp these and address them to yourself all the Editor has to do is tick the relevant box.

They do not have to waste time writing you a letter and they see that you are professional in your attitude to writing.

SUBMISSION ACKNOWLEDGEMENT

From: **Publication:**

Regarding:

We have received the submission referred to above and wish you to know:

- ☐ **It has been accepted, subject to editing**
- ☐ **We plan to use the material in our.................issue**
- ☐ **It is retained pending an editorial decision**
- ☐ **We consider your material unsuitable for our publication**

Signed .... **Title** .... **Date** ....

EDITORIAL OFFER RESPONSE

From: Publication:

Regarding:

We have pleasure in indicating our interest:

☐ Yes, go ahead with the series/article(s) ☐ 1; ☐ 2; ☐ 3; ☐ 4; ☐ 5; ☐ 6.

☐ We'll consider .... words ☐ Date required ....

Send us: ☐ Black and white prints ☐ Colour transparencies

We pay: : Per 100 words : Per black and white print : Per transparency

We pay: ☐ On acceptance ☐ Following publication

☐ Overstocked: try us again in .... months ☐ Sorry, it is not for us

Special notes:

Date: Signed ....

This card is not a contract. Signatory wishes to consider the material offered and may subsequently reject it without cost.

Timing is the essence in submitting ideas. Most magazines have a 'lead' time of three months or more. This is an important fact to remember when suggesting Seasonal and Anniversary features.

The weeklies start thinking about April features in January but the monthlies are by then thinking about features for their July issue. If you want to write an article relating to Christmas for instance, you must submit it to the editor of a weekly magazine in September and a monthly magazine in June.

Bearing in mind your feature may well lie around on the 'slush pile' for several weeks before it is even looked at, then you really do have to plan ahead.

Once you have sent a manuscript off to a magazine, unless it is a definite commission, the best thing to do is to forget about it and get on with the next one.

It could be months before you get a reply, if at all. Whatever happens, do not telephone the editor after a week or two and ask what has happened to it because you will only antagonise them and perhaps jeopardise your chances of future acceptances from that magazine.

I once wrote to *The Lady* after only four weeks asking what had happened to my article and the result was I received it back by first post the next morning, with a printed rejection slip.

It is useful to keep a record of where you send your feature with the date of posting, and the date they accept or reject the piece. It is also useful to note the date of publication of the magazine it is appearing in, providing they give you a date.

This is most important when payment is on publication, as it is with most magazines, as it enables you to budget properly and more important, chase up the accounts department if you don't receive your cheque a month after the article has appeared.

I use a *Writer's Diary-Almanac* published by Know-How Publications which has a Manuscript Tracker in the front. It also contains relevant dates of anniversaries throughout the year plus the 'lead time' to send them to magazines.

It is important to get a good accountant to sort out your tax, because you will no doubt take on part-time jobs to supplement your income and these jobs mostly work on the PAYE system. My accountant is driven mad by my dual accounts for tennis coaching and journalism, as well as the odd payslips for the temporary part time jobs I take when I hit financial difficulties.

The most important thing when contacting the markets that take your fancy is to believe in yourself. If you don't believe your writing is any good it will show in your article. Even when the future seems bleak and you feel you are never going to make it, you must develop an unwavering faith that you are going to get there, and one day that phone call will come from a national magazine and you will see your name in print.

WE ALL MAKE MISTAKES

One thing I found lacking in all the books I read when I first started in journalism was, no-one ever admitted they had made a mistake.

I made several when I started, not the least being I dashed off to interview every celebrity I could grab hold of without giving a thought where I would sell the story.

Consequently I have a box full of 'scoops' I couldn't sell and a group of famous people wondering whatever happened to the scatty girl who nervously sat with a microphone in her hand, and promised they would see their story in print.

Luckily they are all very nice and have never asked where the feature appeared.

Nerves can play a big part in your interviewing technique when you first start. I clearly remember doing a lunchtime interview with Ted Rogers in the office of the Publicity Officer of Eastbourne Theatres.

I was the proud owner of a new tape recorder and microphone that I had purchased at a car boot sale (I was going through one of my financial crises at the time) and it looked much more professional than my little voice recorder I kept in my bag.

Ted did a wonderful interview and I said "I'll just check it" and the tape was blank. I wanted the floor to open up and swallow me up then and there but Ted just turned to me and said "we'll just do it again".

Some mistakes are more costly, and are made through inexperience and I would like to pass on two experiences I suffered through my own stupidity, in the hope it will save some other writer the heartbreak I went through.

I was going through a period of no replies, not even rejections, and I flipped through the *Writer's Handbook* to the page of Agents. I found one who handled journalism and supplied some of the top womens magazines.

He said he could not take on any more clients, but gave me another name. This agent was a one-man business and did not appear in any of the *Writer's Handbooks*, but I telephoned him and he took me out to lunch.

He gave me great hopes for the future and asked me to supply all my material to him as soon as I had written it. He gave me no written details of his terms and conditions, but I did not care, I now had an Agent.

For a year I sent everything I wrote to him and to no-one else. When the South African Cricket Team arrived in England I obtained an exclusive interview with Dr Ali Bacher and several members of the team and my agent said he would send it to South Africa. He also told me the *Daily Telegraph* were 'very keen'. My excitement nearly shot me through the roof.

The Kimberly Dell article, reproduced earlier, was going to be accepted by *Take A Break*, he said, but he was going on holiday so he could do nothing until he returned.

I telephoned *Take A Break* to ask what photographs they required, and they had never heard of me. I then wrote to the *Daily Telegraph* and found out they knew nothing about my cricket feature.

By then I had become a temporary member of the NUJ and I telephoned them for advice.

"Never give any of your work to an Agent unless you have a written agreement showing you their terms and conditions," they said, but I told them it was too late as he not only had my manuscripts, of which I had kept copies, but he had the originals of all my colour transparencies.

With the help of the NUJ I eventually had my work returned and discovered the manuscripts were nearly all in pristine condition, they had never been submitted anywhere. I cried with frustration at the thought of all that wasted work, but my 'agent' had the last word. One feature he failed to return as he told me he had sold it to a magazine but had now withdrawn it, and he was awaiting its return.

People told me not believe him, he was just twisting the knife, but I will never know as he refused to tell me the name of the magazine.

I do not have an agent now as many experienced journalists tell me I don't need one, and I prefer to keep my hard-earned fees rather than giving a commission to someone who will do what I can do myself. Fiction is a completely different ball game and there an agent is the key to the door.

The second mistake I made was more recent and far more costly. I had an idea to write a book about a famous ocean liner and the publisher I suggested it to liked the sound of it.

I wrote to the shipping company and told them what I intended to do and subsequently telephoned the Marketing Department who told me verbally there was no problem as far as they were concerned, and to go ahead.

I certainly did go ahead, spending almost one hundred pounds on posting letters and sending faxes all over the world.

I drove hundreds of miles interviewing people who had travelled in her and took many photographs which I had printed in a large format ready for publication.

All the time I kept the shipping company informed of my movements and said how well the book was going.

It was only when a previous Captain, highly respected in the company, came into the picture did they intervene. I got a letter informing me they were going to produce their own book about the liner and I could not have any support from them. No access to the library and no advertisements in their passengers' newspapers.

Of course everyone told me I should have got agreement in writing, but it is easy to realise that in hindsight. Carried away by the euphoria of the project you do not think clearly and if I can prevent someone else from falling into the traps I fell into with such ease, then I will have achieved one of the aims I set out to reach when I began this book.

HOW WILL I SURVIVE?

The answer is, if you want to take your writing seriously, with difficulty. There is no easy road to fame and fortune for a freelance journalist, and you may think the two hundred odd pounds you get for your one thousand word article is a fortune, especially if you have been earning ten or fifteen pounds for writing odd bits for your local paper.

But put that against your expenses, typing paper, ribbons, discs, photocopying, tapes for your recording machine, films for your camera, the cost of developing and printing your photographs, plus travelling expenses to and from your interviews before you even begin to add up the cost of postage, and you will be lucky to break even, let alone make a profit.

So what do you do; you cannot give up writing for writing is your life. Or it should be if you want to succeed.

You do as I do and take whatever part time job you can to supplement your income. I have worked on a stud farm mucking out Arab race horses, washed up in a pub kitchen, delivered papers round the village, been an agent for books and theatrical mementoes and worked in my village shop.

Luckily I am a qualified secretary and a Licensed Tennis Coach so I do have two other alternative forms of employment, but working in an office is not conducive to being a writer.

More than once one of my bosses has caught me surreptitiously typing out an idea on the office typewriter and one even asked me if I would like an hour off each day to do my own work.

If you are an Olympic athlete employers will bend over backwards to support your efforts to succeed, but they are surprisingly unsympathetic towards budding Jeffrey Archers.

Nothing is more frustrating than to be working on a project and find you have to pack up your typewriter to go and stand behind a counter all afternoon, but needs must. Of all the jobs I have undertaken, working in a shop part time in the afternoons is the most useful complement to writing I have found. You see a variety of characters coming in and out, and it if is a paper shop it does give you a chance to study the latest magazines.

The other part time position that pays well and can be convenient to a writer is Market Research interviewing. A number of companies always advertise for people to work for them, and you can choose the number of days you wish to work every week. You can also be unavailable for work if you have an important interview coming up.

Some firms are reluctant to take you on if you say you are a journalist, as that is one of the barred professions when it comes to finding interviewees, but if you tell them you are a features writer there is no problem. The pay for trained interviewers is good and will keep you going provided you are available for as many jobs as you can possibly fit in with your writing every month.

Again, you meet a very interesting variety of people and by knocking on doors or stopping people in the street it greatly improves both your confidence and interviewing technique.

Once you have established yourself, you can start doing Writing Workshops and passing on your expertise to budding students. The Federation of Womens Institutes also welcomes Guest Speakers, but there is an 'audition' procedure you have to go through and these auditions are held twice a year, in the Spring and Autumn. If you pass this test and get into the *Speakers' Handbook*, the average fee is £22 to £25 per talk plus travelling so it is quite a lucrative earner.

Throughout history writers are reputed to have starved in garrets, never knowing where the next crust was coming from, and things have not changed much, but they have an inner strength that keeps them going and although very few become millionaires they are a happy band of dedicated people and I am proud to be one of them.

SPECIALISATIONS

Once you have gained your confidence, you may wish to specialise. You might have a subject that is dear to your heart and you want to write about that, although there is a danger if you feel very strongly about a controversial subject like politics or religion it could come over in your writing.

Articles must not preach, and if you want to voice your own opinions it must be done in such a way that it won't antagonise the readers and alienate them from your feature before they get half way through.

If you are a nationally renowned columnist you might get away with very strong personal views, but for a writer unknown to the general public it could well put a premature end to your career before it has begun. Editors shy away from anything controversial and will reject it out of hand.

Everyone is an expert in a certain field, even if they do not realise it. Perhaps you are a keen gardener, if so there are many specialist gardening magazines. If photography is your forte, magazines such as *Amateur Photographer*, *Photo Answers* and *Photo Technique* are always asking readers to submit articles and photographs, as well as running regular competitions.

Computer buffs have a great chance of getting an article published, and if your hobby is more unusual like Carp Fishing, making dolls house furniture or making wonderful figures out of papier mache the chances of acceptance are even greater.

A number of womens magazines run 'Readers Stories' and pay well for them, although they may prefer to get one of their own staff journalists to write them up, but it is all money in the bank and you are allowed to say you are a journalist in the feature, so your name will get around.

I chose to specialise in theatre because I worked on the administration side of theatre since my teens. As a secretary at one of the top repertory theatres in the country I used to socialise with some of the 'names' I interview today so they hold no terror for me.

It may sound glamorous to be a theatre critic, but you really have to love the theatre to do this job, as it can involve going to see something three or four times a week. Some of the assignments you get make you the envy of your friends, such as the chance to see Anthony Newley's brilliant performance as *Scrooge*, but more often than not the paper will send you into the depths of the country to see some dreadful amateur production which you have to write about afterwards without offending the entire population of the village.

Photo: Amanda Wilkins

You have to learn to be constructive in your criticism, and not make personal remarks about the actors. Not only could both you and the paper be sued for libel if you denigrate the actor rather than his performance, the producing management can request that you are not sent to cover any of their shows again.

If you are an established theatre critic your editor is unlikely to take any notice of such requests, but if you are just starting on the lowest rung of the ladder it is likely you will not be sent to see another show.

After a young man was caught out in London going to see every West End show on the pretence he was covering them for a certain magazine, theatres are getting much more stringent about issuing press tickets and invitations to press calls, which often involve a free lunch.

Each and every press ticket they give away is one ticket they cannot sell, so it is often necessary to get your editor to inform the theatre in writing you are a bona fide critic covering the show for them.

When I first started covering Eastbourne Theatres I had to convince not only the Director of Entertainment, but the other critics who regularly attended the shows that I was doing a serious job, and not just there for the free tickets.

It took me nearly three years to establish myself, but two of the critics who were suspicious of me to start with have now become my closest friends. They are also both very experienced journalists and have been a great help to me over the years.

Don't go charging in with an air of arrogance and antagonise your colleagues. Listen to their advice from the beginning and learn by your mistakes. When I covered the press call for *Aspects of Love* I took a photograph of the two stars set up by the *Eastbourne Gazette and Herald*. My photograph appeared in the *Sussex Express* the day before the Eastbourne paper was due to come out and they had to scrap their picture.

The next time I met their Chief Photographer he pointed this out to me and I appreciated his advice. I also made sure I did not make the same mistake again. I did it through ignorance and it is only by heeding the information given to you by your more experienced colleagues you learn for the future.

It is not difficult to become a theatre critic, if that is where your talent lies. Your local paper would most probably welcome an offer to cover the shows in the area if you are prepared to work for the ticket and little or no pay.

It is unlikely you will be sent to cover the Royal Shakespeare Company straight away, but there are a myriad of amateur societies who all want to see their show written up in the local paper. The editor will be keen to include it in his paper, as he knows full well it will guarantee sales to each and every member of the society whose name is mentioned in the report, but his hard-pressed staff reporters cannot possibly cover every show.

Amateur productions provide an excellent grounding in theatre criticism. It is perfectly acceptable to criticise a professional actor's performance if you genuinely think it is bad, and not just because you dislike that particular actor. It is a different ball game to destroy performances by amateurs who do perhaps one or two productions a year, fitting in rehearsals with their full time jobs.

They do these shows for fun, building the set, making the costumes and providing entertainment for a village which may well never see live theatre. So what if the set falls down or your local postman forgets his words, this all adds to the fun of the evening and there is no necessity to mention this in your review. Most societies can only manage two rehearsals a week, until the actual week of the production, so how can they possibly be as good as your professional actor and actress who do this every day of their lives, rehearsing for months from morning to night. If you really cannot find anything good to say about the production, which is very unusual, then praise the set, the costumes and the hard work the society has put into getting it on to the stage at all.

A much more difficult field to get into is Sports Journalism. A Sports Reporter on a newspaper, even a small local edition, has to cover every single sport and it is very unlikely, without proper training, you are going to be able to do that.

If you do specialise in one particular sport, mine is tennis, you can write a report for the paper, but it is unlikely you will get either any pay for the piece or a by-line (your name under the article) unless you particularly ask for it. The feature will go to the Sports Editor who will re-write it in his own style and cut it according to the space he has got in that days/week's edition.

There are specialist magazines for the different sports, but they have their own staff reporters, and if they take freelance features at all, they are more likely to use a piece by one of the renowned sports reporters who write for the nationals, like John Parsons, the Tennis Correspondent for the *Daily Telegraph*.

To cover the events you need to get Press Accreditation, otherwise you are unable to attend any interviews, or get near the action to describe it properly.

This involves writing to the Press Officer for the event who will send you a long and sometimes complicated form to fill in. Even if you are a freelance, you will need to say which publication you are covering the event for and places like Wimbledon won't even consider freelances of any kind.

To get Accreditation for the French Open Tennis Championships you have to attach a letter written by the editor of the publication you are covering them for; to say you are just working for them is not enough.

To get 'exclusive interviews' you will almost certainly need a press card. I was extremely lucky to get an interview with His Royal Highness the Duke of Edinburgh this year when he came to Brighton to compete in the Brighton Driving Trials. I had to apply through the Buckingham Palace Press Office and it involved quite a lengthy correspondence.

There were two reasons why the interview was granted: one because I have acted as a Hazard Steward at the Driving trials for a number of years and Prince Philip knew I had a genuine interest in carriage driving; and the second was I held an NUJ Press Card where my name is lodged at New Scotland Yard, so the Press Office was able to check up on me for security reasons.

BROADCASTING

It may be that written journalism is not enough, and if you are an extrovert like me you want to expand your career into broadcasting. I cannot honestly remember when I did my first radio broadcast, as I started reporting on tennis as Publicity Officer for Sussex Lawn Tennis Association many years ago.

I do know I originally started in Hospital Radio in Plymouth, running my own entertainments programme and that is a very good place to cut your teeth. With so many community radio stations springing up, and seasonal stations like *Christmas Radio* that get licences for short periods there are plenty of opportunities to start on a new career.

Your local radio station will welcome offers of phoned in reports on sporting or other events of interest to the listeners, which was how I started at BBC *Southern Counties Radio.* Nothing is more exciting, or nervewracking, than to be given your time slot to ring in so that your report can go out live.

You sit with one eye on the event you are watching and one eye on your watch, terrified of being late. If you are in a public place, such as a tennis club as I was for the Sussex Senior Championships, the chances are there will be only one phone and if someone is using it at your allotted time you really are in trouble.

This happened to me on Finals Day, and I had great difficulty in explaining to the irate gentleman whose call I had interrupted that I just had to use the phone otherwise I would miss my slot.

If one particular station gets to know you, the chances are that they will be willing to give you more work. I got my weekly theatre chat show by introducing myself to the presenter I had worked with at a distance, reporting on tennis. He was at a BBC *Southern Counties Radio* Road Show and my luck was in that day, as it just so happened he had a producer with him who had responsibility for Arts programmes.

I asked if I could do some theatre reviews and he took my name and number. I got a call several weeks later asking me to drive to the studio for an 11.0 p.m. half hour chat show. Once I had established I did not have to drive to their headquarters in Guildford, a considerable distance from my home, I readily agreed to do a weekly drive to Eastbourne.

I am unable to say anything about television, as this is not a medium I have ever tried to get into, and I am not sure I would want to. When the Meridian News Feature programme covered an event at the Southdown Club in Lewes they interviewed me and when I saw the replay of what I looked like, I was not impressed.

If you wish to write for radio and television there are a number of excellent books written on the subject. My favourite television guideline is William Smethurst's *How To Write For Television* in the *How To* series, and Rosemary Horstmann's *Writing For Radio*, published by A & C Black is full of helpful information.

If you do stray into these fields, prepare for a long wait. The BBC Radio Script Department receives a vast number of scripts, and only make decisions twice a year. When the pile gets too big they shut the doors of the Script Department and won't accept any more submissions.

When I wrote to *The Archers* Production Office for a Writer's Pack as recommended in Rosemary's book, I waited a year to receive it. I was given a sample script to write and told to send it back quickly as, if accepted, I would have to work to very tight deadlines. Almost another year on I still have not been told whether I have passed the test.

There are many good books about writing fiction and I am not going to expand on this at all. I cannot write fiction, I have tried. I have two novels under my belt which have done the rounds of the publishers, but all they have proved is I can write 56,000 words.

If romantic fiction is your forte Mills and Boon provide excellent guidelines and a tape. I am quite happy sticking to my Celebrity Interviews and Theatre Reviews. I am hoping by writing this book I will have encouraged you to carry on writing and if I have helped some budding writer get started, or stopped them from giving up, then I will have achieved my aim.

Appendix A

Celebrity Interviews

THE DUKE WHO LOVES HIS DRIVING

In this Exclusive Interview, His Royal Highness the Duke of Edinburgh gives a rare insight into how he became involved in the sport he loves.

One person who will certainly enjoy the Horse Pageant due to be held at Royal Ascot to celebrate the Golden Wedding of her Majesty the Queen and His Royal Highness the Duke of Edinburgh, is His Royal Highness himself.

For Prince Philip's passion in life is Carriage Driving. It takes him away from the pressures of his formal duties and enables him to compete on equal terms with the other drivers.

A popular figure with his fellow competitors, he modestly disagrees with them that it was entirely due to him Horse Driving Trials were introduced to this country.

"I became interested in carriage driving in 1968 while I was President of the International Equestrian Federation," he says. "I discovered that there were several driving events taking place on the continent, but each event was conducted under its own rules. Since it is the FEI that writes the International rules for other equestrian sports, I thought that carriage driving should also have its own international rules so that all organisers, officials and competitors at International events would act in the same way.

"I found a lot of interest, and Colonel Mike Ansell chaired the Committee. The first International event in the U.K. was held at Windsor in 1970 and the first European Championships were held in Hungary in 1971. Germany staged the first World Championships in 1972 and I attended them both in my capacity as President of the FEI."

Carriage Driving is not a sport for the faint-hearted, and Prince Philip did not take it up until he was at an age when most people are thinking about retirement.

"I started driving in 1972 after giving up polo when I reached the age of 50 in 1971, and I learnt partly at Windsor and partly at Balmoral. I began teaching myself by reading Max Pape's book in German."

To someone who finds it difficult to learn even schoolgirl French, I found it amazing that someone could master the intricacies of carriage driving from a book published in another language, but that is the sort of man His Royal Highness is.

Prince Philip now drives a team of Fell ponies owned by Her Majesty the Queen, but I asked him about the first team he ever drove.

"I started driving a pair of horses from the Royal Mews at Windsor in the Spring of 1972 and then during the Autumn I put a team of stalking ponies together at Balmoral. They knew as little about going as a team as I did about driving one.

"The following January, Sir John Miller, then the Crown Equerry, let me have five Cleveland Bay horses from the Mews and persuaded Tommy Thompson, recently retired as Riding Master of the Household Cavalry and an accomplished team driver, to take charge as my Head Groom. He was an accomplished horse master and taught me a lot about driving a four in hand.

"My first driving event was at Lowther in May 1973 when I came fourth out of ten competitors and the second event was as an individual in the European Championships at the Royal Windsor Horse Show, when I was forced to retire at the end of the cross country with a damaged carriage but I finished seventeenth out of nineteen competitors overall."

Photo: Amanda Wilkins

For several years Prince Philip drove his famous teams of Cleveland Bays and I asked him if he noticed a marked difference in driving a team of ponies under 14.2 hands.

"The whole pony outfit is smaller and takes up less room in the obstacles, but, as they have shorter strides, you appear to have to drive them faster to make the same time as horses. My Cleveland Bay x Oldenburg horses were brilliant at dressage (out of 80 starts in 13 years I won 33 of the dressage competitions).

"Fell ponies are very willing to do the dressage tests accurately, but their action and conformation cannot compete with the Welsh ponies for 'style'. While it might be considered easier to drive a team of ponies, that does not mean it is any easier to win!"

A regular competitor at the Brighton Horse Driving Trials held annually in May, last year His Royal Highness was driving a beautifully matched team comprising Balmoral Myrtle (nearside leader) Balmoral Jane (Offside leader) Balmoral Carrick (nearside wheeler) and Dean Fireflight (offside wheeler). They were lying in third place after the Marathon but gave a near-perfect round in the cones section on the final day to finish in second place overall.

The Duke of Edinburgh's Head Coachman, Micky Flynn, was also the recipient of the Len Brunt Cup which is presented annually for the best-kept stabling at the Trials.

At 75 the Duke of Edinburgh recognises that he will need to retire before long, but he hopes he might continue to be associated with the sport as a judge. He is an inspiration to many of the younger drivers and he has also generated an interest in the sport wherever he is competing.

By initiating the formulation of rules for this equestrian sport, which is modelled on the ridden Three Day Event, he has brought us an exciting triathlon for horses which tests the overall versatility of the driven horse.

The driven dressage, perhaps better described as 'compulsory figures' remains an enigma to many spectators, but the cross country marathon of some fifteen miles, which usually includes eight special obstacles, is very exciting to watch, and the cone driving, which equates with the show jumping phase of the ridden event, is a magnificent spectacle when the best livery is worn.

With the current popularity of films such as 'Sense and Sensibility' Horse driving trials gives members of the public an opportunity to see open carriages being actually driven at close quarters.

Further information on Carriage Driving Events, and the Supporters Club may be obtained from the Horse Driving Trials Office, Manor House Farm, Bascote, Near Leamington Spa, Warwickshire CV33 ODX.

Commissioned by The Tatler for their 1997 Verve Cliquot Handbook to the Season.

MR MOONLIGHT - and his leading lady

At the top of the ladder for more than four decades, Frankie Vaughan is still wowing the audiences. AMANDA WILKINS finds out what keeps him going.

Their love affair has lasted nearly half a century and defies the age old myth that showbusiness marriages never endure.

Frankie Vaughan has been married to Stella for 43 years and he knew the instant he met her he was going to marry her.

"It was so simple," he says, "because I just fell in love with her. I had met the girl of my life and the first night I met her I said "I want you to be my girlfriend - forever. And that was it."

One word sums up Frankie Vaughan - charisma. Within five minutes of walking on to the stage at the Theatre Royal in Brighton he has the audience eating out of the palm of his hand.

So how did this theatrical phenomenon begin? He began his career at the Kingston Empire in 1950 - which made him 22 before he is reported to have made his 'professional debut'. I asked him "Why so late?"

"Truthfully," he says, "I was going to be a teacher before I came into showbusiness.

"When I was in the Forces I was in a corvette finishing up in Malta and I used to sing with Maltese bands in Valetta and in hotels round the island.

"People got to know me as a singer and I was earning 25 shillings a day, which was fantastic money. It was good enough for me to think I might need to make a few bob one day.

"When I came out of the army I was within a week of being 21. I had no aspirations to be a singer; I had met Stella and decided I wanted to get married so I went back to college as a student teacher. I had a teaching diploma so I could either teach full-time, or teach and do commercial art as well. I used to be a good artist.

"I was trying to make up my mind what to do when the Leeds student rag revue came up. Because I was known around the town as a bit of a jazz singer, I was asked to audition. The show went on at the Leeds Empire, twice nightly, which was a very big deal. So I went in the show and thoroughly enjoyed it.

"I was creating my own fans in Leeds," he says, "which was fantastic. Keith Waterhouse wrote in the Yorkshire Post 'this boy should go into showbusiness'.

"I was very flattered and just after that I appeared with Harry Parry and his band at the Leeds City Variety. I filled in for his jazz singer for a week as she had been taken ill, and of course, I was the local hero. As a result I was asked by Barney Colehan to see him at the BBC in Leeds to talk about going showbusiness.

"But at the same time I entered a national competition to design a stand for a furniture exhibition at Earl's Court - and I won! Keith

Waterhouse wrote in the Yorkshire Post 'Local boy makes good again' and I had to go to London to collect my prize - which was 35 guineas.

"I told Stella: 'I think commercial art is what I should go in for', but I took with me to London a letter of introduction from Barney Colehan to the Bernard Delfont Agency, in case things didn't work out."

Photo: Amanda Wilkins

Things did not work out for Frank Abelson, as he was then, in the world of commercial art. After collecting his prize money he went round the agencies trying to become a commercial artist, but nothing happened. Had he succeeded, Frankie Vaughan would never have been born.

"I decided to go and see the Delfont Agency," he says, "but it took me three attempts to get to see Billy Marsh. When I did, he asked me 'Why do you want to be a singer?' and I told him "Well I can sing, I am a very good singer."

There is no hint of conceit in his voice. He tells it as if it were the most natural reply.

"So Billy Marsh told me to put an act together and he'd give me a ten-minute spot in the Jimmy Wheeler Show the following Monday. If it was any good, he'd keep me for the week.

"He gave me ten shillings which he said would see me through the week and told me if I went down Archer Street I could get a pianist for five shillings.

"I got a pianist, put an act together and I stopped the show! I was called into Bernard Delfont's office and they said they didn't know what to do with me. It had never happened before."

Frank Abelson was a big hit but he was told it was not a good stage name and he had to think of something new.

"I discussed it with my mother and sisters - and Stella, of course - and we decided it had to be Frankie, but Frankie what?

"My Russian-born grandmother was there and she said to me, "Well, you will always be my number vorn - so there it was, Frankie Vaughan. Because I was her number 'vaughan' grandchild!"

Frankie Vaughan has been stopping the show ever since. He has appeared in theatres, cabaret and television all over the world and has made many films including 'Let's Make Love' with Marilyn Monroe, for whom he has nothing but praise.

"She was beautiful," he says. "A wonderful artist. In front of the cameras she came alive like no-one else, but she couldn't believe anyone could love her for herself."

In his current show he sings a song which just about sums her up.

"It's called 'Incredibly Romantic' and I find it is the best way of explaining the lady. The words just about describe her perfectly."

But his favourite leading lady is the late Dame Anna Neagle.

"Without a doubt," he says. "She was my inspiration for films. She was fantastic. Can you imagine, she wanted me to be her first star in her first production, 'These Dangerous Years' - her husband directed it and she produced it.

"It won me my first acting award - The Picturegoers Award of the Year. Then we appeared together in 'The Lady is a Square' which was a lot of fun because I met Anthony Newley and a great team of actors and actresses and Anna was my leading lady."

Every one of Frankie's fans in the audience at the Saturday matinee I attended wishes they were his leading lady, and there are squeals of delight when he does the high kicks that have become his trademark.

His kicks are still as high - not bad for someone who is 66, and who underwent major heart surgery less than two years ago. Frankie says it was Stella who saved his life.

"We had a couple of days break during the 16-week season in Blackpool," he says, "in which time Stella insisted I had the pain in my back checked.

"I saw a specialist and he said there was nothing to worry about. I had a small lump, a pressure point on the aorta but it was all right. Stella wasn't satisfied and I had a full scan and when they sent it to the John Ratcliffe Hospital they rushed me in immediately. It was like a tyre and it had burst inside: It was hitting the outside wall. Had that gone I wouldn't be here now."

Away from the stage, he still does a lot of work for charity, especially for the Boys' Clubs, for which he was rewarded with an OBE in 1965.

But it is with his family that he is happiest. His eldest son David is a DJ and runs an English-speaking station out in the former Yugoslavia. Younger son Andrew is an actor and musician and can currently be seen in the Babycham advertisements on television as the face in the bubble singing Hey Big Spender. Daughter Susan is married and has two children, Lillie Victoria and James Michael.

But it is Stella's devoted support that has kept Frankie going and kept him at the top through four marvellous decades.

Published in Yours Magazine, February 1995

AFTER HOLLYWOOD...EASTBOURNE

AMANDA WILKINS interviews MICHAEL PRAED, star of Dynasty, Robin of Sherwood and Riders

Dynasty star Michael Praed is looking forward to playing the Congress Theatre in Eastbourne in Barry Manilow's Copacabana in June, as his first week coincides with the Direct Line International Womens Tennis Championships.

Photo: Supplied by Public Eye

Michael loves tennis, both watching it and playing it, but he is finding accommodation for the first week a problem as everything is booked up.

"I would like to bring my family down as we play for three weeks from June 18 but finding anything near the theatre during Tennis Week is proving pretty impossible," he says.

"It is really bizarre coming back to Eastbourne, as I went to Eastbourne College from the age of eight to 18 and it was about half a mile up the road there that I decided to become an actor." We are sitting in the upper foyer of the Congress Theatre, overlooking the college, and Michael is pointing to Carlisle Road.

"I remember it very clearly indeed because we had just taken our mock O-levels and one of the teachers came up and said 'We need to know what you want to do for A-level' and I hadn't even taken my O-levels yet.

"But they needed to know at that time how many science students they might have and how many arts-based students, and I realised that what A-levels you do influence to a large extent what degree you do and that influences what sphere you want to go into, and I knew I had to think about this very carefully. My father had always said ' Be very careful about this choice' and I thought 'What do I really want to do?'

"The extraordinary thing about Eastbourne College is they not only take extracurricular activities very seriously, the standard is very good. They used to put on a play a term, which takes some effort".

Michael's father's advice paid off and he trained at the Guildhall School of Music and Drama. His first professional job was at the Nuffield Theatre, Southampton in 'The Tempest', when he played a sprite or a fairy ("I can't remember which") and a Bosun and various assorted roles, and he made his west End debut at the Theatre Royal, Drury Lane, when he played Frederick in 'The Pirates of Penzance'.

Michael is probably best known for his role of Prince Michael of Moldavia in 'Dynasty', a role he played for two years, and I asked him how he was selected for the part.

"I'd just done a show on Broadway and I was asked if I'd like to fly to Hollywood and meet some people, so I said 'OK' and that's really how it happened."

I had to ask him what it was like working with Joan Collins and he gave a diplomatic reply "It's pretty much the same as working with any other multi-talented actress. It's difficult to paraphrase sort of two years of your life and also it was a very long time ago. In addition, the show had been running quite a few years before I arrived. But she's ravishingly beautiful and she's a lovely, lovely lady.

Besides playing the title role in two series of 'Robin of Sherwood' for HTV, the other role which made Michael a household name in Britain is that of Jake in the television adaptation of Jilly Cooper's novel 'Riders'. He has a few bad memories about playing this part as he says he nearly got killed on a horse during the recording, which was a salutary experience. "I'd never really ridden before. When I played Robin Hood I was given a crash course, but I used to hang on to the saddle for dear life. When we did 'Riders' we had to jump but I didn't know there is a vast difference to just being able to ride and being able to jump.

"When we did 'Riders' they got the Household Cavalry to teach us how to jump, which was the most extraordinary experience because they have one method of teaching people and they have exquisite animals. They are so well trained and they will do what you ask them to do, so for that purpose they are great horses and within a couple of weeks we were jumping five feet.

"We had doubles as well, but every single fence you see, we are doing it and I took a bad tumble."

In 'Copacabana' Michael plays the lead role of the charismatic bartender Tony and he is thoroughly enjoying the show. He is touring throughout the UK until December 14, after which he is hoping to return to America. But his main thought after I met him was to find somewhere to stay in Eastbourne so that his ex-dancer wife Karen and his two children, Gabriel and Frankie, can join him for the three week run.

Photo: Amanda Wilkins

Published in The Buzz, June 1996

PROFILE - CAMERON MACKINTOSH. THE MUSIC MAN.

Theatre's newest knight, Sir Cameron Mackintosh, has achieved outstanding success by anyone's terms. He has done this with a combination of determination and enthusiasm, as well as a genuine eye for great musicals.

The newly beknighted Sir Cameron Mackintosh has established himself as one of the most successful theatre producers of all time. With over 300 productions to his credit, and six shows currently playing in the west End - Cats, Five Guys Names Moe, Les Miserables, Miss Saigon, Oliver and The Phantom of the Opera - his name is a byword for blockbusting musical theatre. He also has some 50 productions running worldwide, two thirds of which are directly under his control, and the rest licensed out. His next show, Martin Guerre, opens in London in June.

Sir Cameron has an infectious enthusiasm for the theatre. He once said he was as excited about it today as when he started, and this enthusiasm rubs off on his staff. Nicholas Allott, who runs his London office, says the success of Cameron Mackintosh Limited is due entirely to Cameron's individuality. Yet he remains modest about his achievements, preferring to remain behind the scenes, and the public who flock to see his shows would probably not recognise him if they passed him in the foyer.

He started at the bottom, working as a stagehand at the Theatre Royal, Drury Lane - now home to one of his most successful productions, Miss Saigon. This was in the mid- sixties, when he was paid just £14 a week. After rent and other expenses, he was left with just £2 to spend on groceries. Fortunately, the fact that he is a reasonably good cook meant he was able to lead a fairly comfortable existence.

Working his way up, in 1965 he became acting assistant stage manager on a national tour of Oliver, and from 1977 onwards he produced several revivals of the original production. He is now co-owner of the rights to Oliver, and his hugely popular production is, of course, running at the London Palladium.

His first venture in the West End, with Anything Goes some twenty years ago, was a disaster, but he was certainly not put off by the experience. He made his first tentative mark on the London scene as a producer after Julian Slade (of Salad Days fame) adapted Arthur Wing Pinero's Trelawny of the Wells into a musical. The show opened in the Bristol Old Vic, where it was a great success, and Cameron obtained the rights to transfer it to London. This was followed by his first international success with Side By Side By Sondheim, the show that gave a hint of his ability to make serious money in the theatre. It cost £6,000 to put on and made £150,000 profit, playing all over the world and establishing Sondheim's reputation in the U.K.

It was in 1981 that the world really knew Cameron Mackintosh had arrived, when he collaborated with Andrew Lloyd Webber on a new musical based on T.S. Eliot's poems from Old Possum's Book of Cats. That show - in case you have been off the planet for the past decade and a half - was called Cats. It was an immediate success, and is still playing to packed houses at the New London Theatre fifteen years later, recently becoming the world's longest running musical.

Andrew Lloyd Webber's attention had been attracted by the success of Cameron's collaboration with the Arts Council to create touring productions of My Fair Lady and Oklahoma. The tour was funded by the Arts Council and various regional authorities, to fill the newly refurbished Palaces and Hippodromes around the country, which were now mainly council owned after lying dark for years. Both shows then came into London, where their success caught Lloyd Webber's eye and sparked off an extremely profitable collaboration, ending with Phantom of the Opera.

Now Cameron is working again with Claude-Michel Schonberg and Alain Boubil, the pair who created Les Miserables and Miss Saigon, to present a new musical. Martin Guerre has its world premiere at London's Prince Edward Theatre on 18 June, with previews from 22 May. After the unlikely success of Les Miserables, now in its eleventh record-breaking year, this looks set to become another hit for the Mackintosh stable.

Based on the true story of a man returning from the wars claiming to be Guerre - although his wife and the community have their doubts - it is a tale of passion, jealousy and deception, set in the time of the French religious wars.

Over the years successes have far outweighed the failures, although there have been one or two. According to Cameron, After Shave - an all-girl review - still brings an astringent glow to his investors' cheeks. Moby Dick, the show he financed which was panned by the critics, is still produced regularly by professional and amateur companies and has its fervent devotees. Today, however, any musical with which he is associated usually has the seal of approval from the general public and is almost guaranteed to reap his investors rich rewards.

Success has ensured the 49 year old impresario will be financially secure for the rest of his life. At the last count his personal fortune was estimated at more than £200 million, and last year he was number 81 on the list of Britain's 500 richest people. The money has enabled him to buy homes in France and New York, as well as the beautiful Nevis Estate at Mallaig in the north west highlands of Scotland. Cameron originally inherited a tiny log cabin there from his aunt Jean, then discovered the 12,000 acre estate was due to be sold and snapped it up.

If he can tear himself away from the work he loves, it is in Mallaig that he hopes eventually to spend more time. He has known the place all his life, and the villagers - who have known him since he was a child - are unphased by his fame and fortune. When he strolls through the breathtaking countryside he can totally relax, and conversation with anyone he meets is more likely to be about the weather than his next production.

Cameron obviously grew up in a creative environment, and this also shows in his two brothers. Robert runs the entertainment division of Firecrest, and not only produces records and shows, but also writes the music, while Nicky owns Mackintosh's restaurant in Chiswick. Their father, Ian, who has sadly just passed away was a jazz trumpeter. Although he gave up the uncertain life of a professional musician after the war to run the family timber business, at 77 he still managed to play at last year's Edinburgh Festival. Both he and their mother Diana, who were together for fifty years, supported and encouraged their sons in their chosen careers.

Diana has helped Cameron out as a typist - unpaid of course, and even invested some of her own money in his early shows.

Such support and faith is natural in a parent, but Diana seems to have had inside information. The story goes that when Cameron was 12 years old, she went to a palmist who told her one of her sons was going to be famous. She knew at once it would be Cameron - probably because aged eight he told her he intended to produce musicals when he grew up. He has certainly fulfilled that palmist's prophesy, but he has done this by sheer hard work and resilience. Unlike many enormously successful people, he remains well-liked and respected for his amiable and generous character as well as for his talent.

It is a mark of the man's generosity of spirit that he insisted that Lionel Bart, who wrote Oliver, be given a stake in the production, despite having sold the rights years before. This is certainly not the sort of gesture routinely expected of people in his position, but would surprise few of the people who know him well. Through his charitable foundation, he gives away huge sums each year to deserving causes - indeed this is one of the reasons for his knighthood.

Cameron is also protective of his actors, and believes in sticking by his principles. The American actors' union initially refused to allow British actor Jonathan Pryce to transfer to Broadway with the London production of Miss Saigon in 1991. Cameron threatened to cancel the show unless they rescinded their ban, even though it would have meant losing millions of pounds. They relented and the show went ahead. His resilience had paid off.

His knighthood is well deserved and warmly welcomed in theatrical circles, but this unassuming maestro of the musical will take it all in his stride and just get on with the job in hand.

Published in Theatre Magazine, March / April 1996

FROM BERNARDO TO BRONTE

Actor George Chakiris is still stirring female hearts in a new leading role.

It is 35 years since heart throb George Chakiris gave his award-winning performance as Bernardo, leader of the Sharks, in the film West Side Story. But you would never think more than three decades have passed when you meet him now.

Perhaps there are a few more lines etched on his face, and his hair is longer, but he is reluctant to reveal his age because, he says "it will spoil the illusion". When pushed, he admits to being 58, then he adds with a laugh "That's not the truth of course".

We met in his dressing room at Eastbourne's Devonshire Park Theatre, where he is playing Mr Rochester in Jane Eyre.

George cannot remember ever making a conscious decision to become an actor, he just fell in love with the movies at an early age. As the son of Greek immigrant parents he lived a fairly nomadic existence during his formative years.

"I was born in Ohio," he says, "but we left there when I was three and went to live in Arizona which is where I was introduced to the cinema. When I was five we moved to Florida, where we stayed until I was nine, then we went back to Arizona. We finally moved to California, where we settled down, when I was 12.

"I went to school wherever we lived, and my father took whatever job he could get to support his family. My parents were very simple people, but wonderful."

His father died in 1968, but his mother will be 92 in October. She lives in Los Angeles, where George has his own house which he shares with a thoroughbred Italian greyhound called Sandy, a cat, two rabbits and a parrot.

"They are all strays. Whenever I go away I have someone come and stay in the house so that they are all comfortable."

His musical career started with his move to California when he joined the choir at St Luke's Episcopal Church in Long Beach and he appeared in the film Song of Love which starred Katherine Hepburn. He had no formal drama training because he says that wasn't the practice on the West Coast of America.

"If I had lived in London I would have known about drama schools. Even if I'd been living in New York I would probably have gone to one, as the acting community there are very aware of the drama schools and the wonderful teachers available. When I was 19, which is the age I started professionally, in California it was the studio system to put people under contract."

A singing and dancing natural, George was soon signed up and appeared in the chorus in film classics such as There's No Business Like Show Business, Brigadoon, Meet Me in Las Vegas and the legendary White Christmas.

"It was such fun," he says. "And a great thrill to be working behind great stars like Bing Crosby, Donald O'Connor, Danny Kaye and Gene Kelly."

He worked on the number 'Diamonds are a Girls Best Friend' in the film Gentlemen Prefer Blondes with Marilyn Monroe, whom he remembers as very professional.

"I never got to speak to her," he says, "but she cared deeply about her work. She never behaved like a star. Whenever there was a cut, instead of going back to her trailer to fix her make-up, she just went right back to her starting position and waited to continue."

Deciding he wanted to work on the New York stage George moved to Manhattan where he slept on a friend's couch. It was a move that was to change his life. He managed to land an audition for the London production of West Side Story and was chosen to play "Riff", the leader of the Jets (Bernardo's deadly rival). It was his first stage role and the start of his meteoric rise to fame. Jerome Robbins, who co-directed and choreographed the film, cast George as Bernardo, leader of the Sharks. By playing both parts George feels he has had the best of both worlds.

"In the theatre version Riff is a slightly better role than Bernardo as he gets to sing 'Cool' and in the stage version the Puerto Rican boys are not involved in the song 'America'. It's a wonderful number and luckily in the film as Bernardo I was able to be part of it."

Unlike many actors who are remembered largely for one role George bears no resentment, although he has done a lot of good work since the film which made his name.

"Bernardo enabled me to work in all parts of the world," he says, "because the film is constantly being shown and re-shown. If I hadn't been in West Side Story I wouldn't be here right now."

It also brought him an Academy Award, and he remembers the Oscar Ceremony as being "wildly exciting".

"You really don't know you've won until they make the announcement," he says. "I was too naive at the time to realise what it meant in a professional way, but I just knew something wonderful had happened."

His dynamic performance also won him a Golden Globe Award and in June 1991 he was awarded the status of 'Officer de l'Ordre des Arts et des Lettres' by the French Minister of Culture. "It was a complete surprise," he says. "I had no idea they were going to give it to me.

"West Side Story was hugely successful in France and played the same theatre on the Champs-Elysees for five years, a record I think no other film has beaten, and they always like me over there."

He has done a lot of work in Europe and starred with Claudia Cardinale in Bebo's Girl in Italy, where he also made The Theft of the Mona Lisa, but George says he does not really mind where he works as long as the script is good.

"The most important thing is the material" he says "If you've got good material then you're ahead of the game, and the second most important thing is to be working with good people in a nice atmosphere."

His favourite medium is live theatre, although he recalls "I really enjoyed working on the TV series Dallas alongside the wonderful Barbara Carrerra - we were villains trying to steal oil from JR. It was such a beautifully run show with a wonderful crew, it was great to work on."

When he finishes Jane Eyre in June, George intends to head back to Los Angeles for a while. "I've been away quite a lot" he says "Last year I was in France making a mini-series called Le Lido for French television and I just want to be at home. I love my family desperately, but I miss Sandy more than anything."

Away from the theatre George likes to spend time with his family and friends. He has never married, although he says he got quite near it a few years ago.

"It was someone I worked with," he says, enigmatically not naming the lady. "But we were both professionals and she went one way and I went the other, but we are still very good friends."

George has loved England since he first opened at London's Haymarket Theatre in 1958 in West Side Story and there is no doubt that he will soon be back. Unless, of course, Japan, France, Italy or anywhere else in Europe where he has a loyal following snaps him up first.

George Charkiris in Jane Eyre. Photo supplied by Charles Vance Productions.

Published in SAGA Magazine June 1996

A LEGEND HOLDS COURT

In an exclusive interview, tennis great Ken Rosewall serves a volley that explains why the fun has gone out of the game today.

Tennis has been his entire life and at 61 going on 20, Ken Rosewall still plays a mean game of tennis.

Partnering a mere "chicken" Hana Mandlikova, 34, they easily won the first ever Legends event at Eastbourne, the week before Wimbledon.

The one-day round robin event, part of the International Ladies Tennis Championships, was made up of four mixed pairs; Tony Roche and Rosie Casals, Ken and Hana, Fred Stolle and Virginia Wade and Owen Davidson and Betty Stove.

The matches provided the appreciative crowd with great entertainment and confirmed what Ken told me when I caught up with him away from the tennis court.

"It was all so different in our day. We played for fun. Like a lot of the old tennis players in Australia in those days from Frank Sedgman on, and certainly in the days of Lew Hoad and Rod Laver, we all came from tennis playing families and I think today there's a big difference.

"There are families who are pushing their children into tennis because they can see that if they become good they can travel and there's the possibility of making a lot of money. We've seen it on the circuit these days, parents who are so pushy without understanding what it's all about."

Ken, born in Sydney, New South Wales, on November 2nd 1934 was the only child of a grocer but both his parents played tennis.

"In those days it was the thing to do in Australia. It was a very cheap game" he said.

"My dad learnt by reading old tennis books, then he taught me. He was in a big retail store for a while, then he got away from that and went into small grocery shops. But they're almost a thing of the past the way big business is dealing these days."

Ken started 'messing about' with a racket when he was four or five and started playing junior tournaments when he was 10 years old.

"In the 13 years and under I was a bit above average," he said, "and fortunately for me so was my compatriot Lew Hoad. We were kind of partners. We both lived in Sydney, in different suburbs and started teaming up in the juniors. We were very competitive and it helped to improve each other's game."

Hoad, who sadly died last year, and Rosewall became known as the "Sydney twins". They both left school at 14 and joined the Slazenger Sporting Goods Company.

"That's the way the game was played in those days. A lot of the leading players had some kind of employment with the sporting goods companies, not that we did a lot of work, I admit.

Photo: Amanda Wilkins

"Part of our agreement was that we were allowed to travel overseas and play with their equipment for about eight months of the year, and for the other three or four months we played special little exhibition matches in and around the areas of Australia which promoted the products of whatever particular company we were part of."

Australian Davis Cup Captain Harry Hopman introduced the "twins" to the team when they were both aged 19 and they received a few shillings a day expenses. Rosewall played in the team until 1956 when he turned professional, but even then he did not make vast amounts of money.

"When I toured with Jack Kramer's professional "tennis circus" I think I was paid about ten bob per match," he recalled. I asked him if he found it galling that today's players can earn so much for winning Grand Slam events when he won just peanuts.

"Not really" he said "I won my first Australian and French titles when I was 18 and I was very excited about having the chance to play tennis and to play off in Finals, so you didn't really know what was ahead of you and you certainly didn't know what was ahead of the game.

"The money has encouraged many more people to play tennis. The game has exploded in every country in the world. When you look at tennis players and rankings, you don't know where they are from or how to pronounce their names. But I do think tennis has been spoilt a little by the different kind of equipment, the style of players and maybe the elimination of the grass court part of the game which was the real tradition, and I am a traditionalist.

"I think there are a lot of us who think it'd be great to be playing now and losing the first round but still picking up £5,000 or whatever."

He's still playing but Ken admits that his days on court may be numbered.

"The ATP (Association of Tennis Professionals) that run the Men's Tour are also trying to do Senior events that have players of 35-45 and over. Unfortunately, I am at the wrong end of the 45 years and over, so with the process of elimination I might just be coming to the end of my play.

"My last year in competitive tennis was about 1978 or 1979 when I was 41 or 42. When you're giving 15 or 20 years to some of the younger players it isn't proving anything. Now it's happening in the "Legends" events, although that, of course, has a doubles format and they pair a younger player with an older player so it works."

Nicknamed "Muscles" because of his comparative frailty of physique, Ken looks much the same as people remember him, although he says he might be a little heavier and quite a lot of steps slower. At five feet seven he was always smaller and less flamboyant than his "twin" Lew Hoad, but he had a tremendous back-court accuracy which he has never lost.

Ken travels with his wife Wilma, who missed his triumph at Eastbourne as she was confined to bed with a heavy cold.

They met 'many many years ago', and were married on October 6th 1956. They celebrate their Ruby Wedding this year. Their two sons are now grown up and have presented them with three grandchildren.

"Our older boy, Brett, who is 37 is an airline pilot with Cathay Pacific and lives with his wife and son in Hong Kong. Glenn is 34 and in the financial market. He lives in Sydney with his wife and two children."

Had the boys taken after their father as far as tennis is concerned?

Ken laughed "They were not really encouraged to do so a great deal because in those early days I was away from home a lot and it was a bit of a struggle, but Glenn's two children play tennis. We were fortunate when I was playing in that we did have a chance to travel a bit and one of the more memorable moments is when we were all together as a family when I played my last Wimbledon Final over 20 years ago."

Although he won the Australian, French and American titles more than once the Wimbledon title has always eluded him. Even though he reached the Final four times, in 1954, 1956, 1970 and 1974. His whole life has been tennis but he has no regrets.

"Even though I am basically retired, when I go home to Australia I don't have any day-to-day business so I am able to work and play with some of the juniors and I am delighted I am still involved with the game."

"Home" is Turramurra, a suburb of Sydney "I live near Tony Roche and John Newcombe. There are quite a few Australian players who live in Sydney now and we are still playing a little bit for fun."

When he can be dragged away from the tennis court, Ken likes to play golf. Officially his handicap is 14 but he admits he wishes he could play to it.

"I'd like to get it down, but I've travelled since I was 17 and that's one of the bugbears of living in Australia. It is the reason why a lot of our golfers and tennis players live in Europe or America - they are closer to the tour and don't have to travel so far."

But Ken obviously loves his country and would like to see more of it. "There are many areas I haven't seen. As a matter of fact my wife and I took a trip to Western Australia, we were in Perth for a few days. Then we went to Broom in North Western Australia, it's quite remote, a lot of pearling is still going on, it was very interesting."

As he went off to practise with Hana he told me he was looking forward to playing Wimbledon again with Fred Stolle. His face lights up when he talks about the prospect of meeting old friends and watching the younger players.

And, even though he is coming to the end of his career in the Legends events, it is hard to believe Ken Rosewall will ever retire. Tennis is his life, it always has been and always will be so long as his legs will carry him across a court.

Published in SAGA Magazine August 1996

LYNNE MCGRANGER - AT HOME & AWAY

You get a surprise when you meet Lynne McGranger. She looks younger and prettier than she does on television in the role that has made her a household name to "Home and Away" fans, that of reformed drunk Irene. She says it is the strong lights that make her look older, and the bright blue eyeshadow doesn't help.

Although she loves performing, it was never her original intention to become a professional actress.

"For some peculiar reason I wanted to be a hairdresser," she says, "although I can't do hair. Then I wanted to be a cookery teacher and I can't cook, so I don't know where I get these ideas from."

Lynne did become a teacher, but it was inevitable she would end up as an actress as she started ballet at the age of five and as a child she used to put on backyard concerts, charging neighbours threepence to come and watch.

"I have a younger sister, but she never had any inclination to perform," she says. "Although she does have a very nice singing voice. I was always a show off. By the age of seven I knew the whole album from "My Fair Lady" by heart and I used to perform all the parts and make friends and neighbours sit through it.

"I was always being told I had a good personality and I think I was like all children, looking for approval. I was quite plump and rather plain so I showed off to compensate. When I was at school I was in the choir and always appeared in the end of year concerts.

"When I left I went on to Teachers College in a small town called Wogga Wogga and became involved in drama there, then there was an amateur Drama Festival in the town in which I played a young Irish girl in Brian Fields play set in Norethern Ireland called "Lovers".

"I got the Best Actress Award and people always laugh when I tell them I won the Wogga Wogga Drama Festival, but that was actually the point when it first occurred to me I might be able to act as it was a straight role, no singing or dancing.

"But I continued with my college training, and at this stage I was doing primary school teaching. At one time I was going to become a Maths and Science teacher, then an English and History teacher. I'm not terribly bright, just terribly confused. I kept changing my mind.

"After three and a half years I came out of college and started teaching and I did last a couple of years, but it didn't take me long to realise I was allergic to children in groups of more than one and I decided teaching was not the way to go.

"I got involved with a theatre workshop which started out of a professional company and I moved out to the West of Sydney where they were based. They asked me to work in a professional production and I had to join Equity, so I sort of did things back to front. I did a few productions for them then I went to drama school for two years, so I didn't really start acting until I was in my late twenties.

"I think this was a bonus for me because I was never beautiful enough when I was young, I never had that TV look, but as I got older I guess I have developed character.

"I didn't do a lot of TV work before "Home and Away", I did a little bit of "Country Practice" which was my first TV, and I had a fifty worder as a nurse in "Flying Doctors", but I must be the only forty year old actress in Australia who has never done "Prisoner Cell Block H. Most of my work was theatre, stand-up comedy, cabaret and straight plays."

So how did Lynne land the part of Irene in "Home and Away", a role which was originally created by Jackie Phillips?

"It's an interesting story actually," she says, "because I was doing a play called "Daily Grind" about two strippers, and yes I did strip down to my G-string, and a very well known producer wanted me and the other girl to audition for a TV series he was doing entitled "The Seven deadly Sins" in one called "Envy". Before I went for the audition I was told the part had been cast, ironically it went to Jackie, the original Irene, but I got a call from Liz Mulliner, the major casting agent in Australia who casts for "Home and away" who said another role had come up in "Seven Deadly Sins" in Gluttony and they wanted me to do it.

"When I went for the audition I had food poisoning and I hadn't eaten for three days, I was so ill I couldn't remember my lines. I was such a mess but I got the role and a fortnight later I got a call from my agent to say Liz Mulliner wanted me for a guest role in "Home and Away" which had the potential to be ongoing.

"When I got the character breakdown I saw it said this 'thin wasted alcoholic' and I knew I had been picked because when Liz saw me I looked like death on legs. Anyway I went for an audition thinking it was going to be a cattle call and I was the only person auditioning. Liz is such a good casting agent that she knew as soon as she saw me she had got the woman.

"I had to get my hair bleached and all of that, and I first started playing Irene in October 1992. I played her for thirteen weeks until February 1993 but when I left the producer asked me if I was interested in coming back and of course I said "Is the Pope a Catholic? Six months later I signed the contract and started coming back, that was August 1993, and I've just re-signed for another two years.

"I love the series and we're like a great big family. Some of the younger ones need a bit of a kick up the bum occasionally, but it really is just great. Emily Symons, who plays Marilyn, is my best friend. She's just wonderful. She's a very funny woman and I just adore her. We have such fun on the set, it's never deadly serious.

"There was one time we were doing a scene in the Beach House with Rosemary, that bloody pig, and Emily was carrying her up the stairs and she pooped. This hard pellet just went boink, boink, down the stairs and we were all shrieking, it's the funniest thing I've seen in my life.

"Another time I was being naughty, I was in the kitchen of the diner out of shot and I had some oranges. I was juggling, which I do very badly, and one went straight into the soup. The man on the boom nearly fell off laughing and I had to walk straight into the diner and act. I had no time to compose myself."

In the series Selina (Tempany Deckert) is like Irene's adopted daughter, but in real life Lynne says she is more like her mother.

"She's seventeen going on forty-seven," she says. "She's so intelligent and witty and bright and sometimes I'll be on the set mucking about and she'll say "Lynne, stop it, you're being naughty again' and I really feel I'm with my mother half the time."

Lynne lives with partner Paul and five year old daughter Clancy in Sydney, where the series is filmed. Paul is a musician and plays keyboards but she says he has been a househusband for two years since she's been doing "Home and Away".

"I couldn't have done without him," she says, "because I'm often home late and I have lines to learn. I can't run a house and a family and do that at the same time.

"The series is never shot in sequence, it is filmed in blocks from Monday to Friday although it is all written chronologically. The outdoor shots are filmed the week before so if I am going into the studio this week I will be filming this week's interiors and next week's outside shots. I learn the scripts in order and hopefully it sticks in, then I have to think 'hang on a minute'. This hasn't happened yet, so I can't be upset, that's got to wait."

Lynne was able to get to England to do her first ever pantomime at Christmas when she played Fairy Bowbells in "Dick Whittington" at Brighton's Dome Theatre. She brought her family with her and took a flat in Hove and she really enjoyed her first English Christmas.

"I've done Childrens Theatre in Australia," she says, "but never traditional pantomime, but I loved doing it because it allowed me to do what I enjoy doing most, acting stupid and singing and dancing a bit."

She would love to return next Christmas but she doesn't think the producers will allow it as they lose everybody from the show.

"We do get four weeks off, but we start filming in mid-January and go through to late September usually without a break, which is a great strain and people are so ill."

The four weeks break gives Lynne a chance to indulge in her main passion, cricket. She has a secret ambition to become a cricket commentator although she says she doesn't really know enough about it.

"I started watching it on television in the early eighties and it was something I gradually got interested in, and now I'm quite fanatical about it. I really love it, particularly when you are winning and it helps when you are considered to be the best in the world."

The other passion is her work. It was her hobby for so long she has to keep pinching herself to realise someone is actually paying her to do it, and she is quite happy about Irene's lack of romantic success in the series.

"I would hate to have a successful relationship," she says. "If I did all I would do is end up making cakes for the diner!"

Commissioned by My Weekly 1996

COAXING COX

With his curly blonde hair and Rover tracksuit Mark Cox is a familiar sight on the tennis scene. As Director of the Rover Junior Tennis Initiative he is always on the lookout for promising young players and Amanda Wilkins checks out the man behind the programme reviving British Tennis.

Mark is one of the most popular characters in tennis and he was one of Britain's most successful players. Between 1969 and 1977 he alternated with Roger Taylor as Britain's number-one with Mark coming out on top 6-4. And he remained in the top three until his retirement in 1961.

But what of the man himself? During a visit to the Southdown Club in Lewes to see the Sussex Junior Closed Championships I took the opportunity to talk to him about his life and career.

Never taking his eyes off the 10 & Under boys quarter-final he was watching, he told me

"I was born in Leicester back in 1943 and my parents were both keen tennis players of good club standard. My father was a Junior County Trialist, which I think was as far as he got, but tennis in those days was very much part and parcel of their social life.

"My father was a draughtsman then, although later he became a Personnel Manager, and the firm he worked for had a very active works club which my parents belonged to so I was virtually brought up with a tennis racket.

"It's hard to say what age I really started playing. I pottered around playing tennis for many years but there were no really serious junior tournaments. I suppose the only junior tournaments were the Under 15 events at Nottingham and Oxford. The game was basically Under 18.

"My father used to coach me and we've still got the book we used - Frank Sedgeman's "Winning Tennis" - with all the bits underlined!

"I was very fortunate because at the age of 13 I was selected to play for the Leicestershire Senior Team and they certainly helped me a lot.

"I went to school in Leicester until I was 15 and then I won a scholarship to Millfield. Then I had a year off and went out to Australia and New Zealand playing tennis on a British team with Stanley Matthews, Graham Stilwell and Roger Taylor.

"When I came back I went to Cambridge and after that I joined a stockbroking firm, but it was obvious to them I was going to be better off playing tennis!

"The idea was when I came back I would spend a few weeks in the office which I did, but it didn't happen very often.

"When Professional Tennis came in I joined World Championship Tennis which was Lamar Hunt's group of sixteen players. I had a contract for three years from 1970 and I played with great players like Laver, Rosewall, Newcombe, Roche and Riessen. I was one of the weakest of the sixteen in fact, but it was great training and experience."

Mark met his wife through tennis who, as Alison Stroud, played at Wimbledon. They have been together for 29 years.

Photo: Amanda Wilkins

"We got married in 1966, just as I finished at University and her playing enabled us to get around the world. we played Mixed Doubles at Wimbledon together and, in fact, won the Husband and Wife Mixed Doubles at the US Championships in 1966". The couple have a son and daughter but both have given up full time tennis for different reasons.

"Stephen probably would have gone into tennis professionally but he has got cardiomyopathy so he has had to give up playing tennis altogether.

"This is an illness affecting the muscle of the heart and Stephen had all sorts of other problems connected with it. Very athletic people get this and it is never discovered until it is too late, so we were very lucky."

He was on a scholarship to an American university where automatic health screening first detected the problem. Fortunately the cardiologist had experience of this and knew what to look for. That was a blessing as they were able to do further tests.

"Stephen has accepted he can't play any more and would like to go into sports psychology and counselling but he has a year's work experience to do so he is still some years from finishing his course at the University of Guildford."

At the moment the cause of cardiomyopathy is unknown and there is no specific treatment so Alison Cox has been actively raising money to set up a fund to research into the illness.

When Mark retired from playing in 1981 he joined the LTA on a part time basis as Davis Cup trainer. In 1987 the Cox family emigrated to New Zealand but things did not work out as they had hoped.

"We did it in a fit of mid-life crisis," he said. "It was like a blood-letting for us but we realised we were British in spirit and wanted to be back home, really.

"We returned in 1988 and moved to Ashtead in Surrey and on the Ist of January 1989 I started working full time for the LTA. My job initially was to try and liaise with the regions and at national level to see what was going on in regional training, and what tennis opportunities there were for young players in Britain."The outcome of it was that I sort of formulated the views that everyone was putting forward, which was really that we had talented young players but they were not getting the opportunities so I put forward a programme and a proposal was received by Rover Cars and they funded it.

"I put it down on paper and Paul Hutchins put it to Rover and we have been very fortunate to have a major British company supporting British tennis in the way they have.

"The feedback we are getting from Europe is good. Coaches are asking what we are doing in Britain. The reality is that we have done nothing unique. We've given many good young players the opportunity to train, work on court, get good coaching, a good competitive programme.

"We look at their fitness, address their diet, teach them to be very much more professional in their attitude and be more geared to performing and improving and we try to give them the resources to achieve these objectives.

"Consequently and not unnaturally those players have got better. We now have a number of very promising players. I think it is probably dangerous to name names, but there are quite a number of young players who are exciting prospects and we are starting to see evidence of that."

As Mark went off with his clipboard to watch another match his enthusiasm never dwindled. Just listening to him talk about his work one gets immersed in his energy which makes one believe that if anyone is going to put the 'great' back into British tennis, Mark Cox is the person.

Published by Tennis Post July 1996

Appendix B

Useful Addresses

Organisations

The Archers
Pebble Mill
Birmingham B5 7QQ
Tel: 0121 414 8400

BAFTA (British Academy of Film and TV Arts)
195 Piccadilly
London WlV OLN
Tel: 0171 734 0022

BBC Radio
Broadcasting House
London WlA lAA
Tel: 0171 580 4468

BBC Television
Television Centre
Wood Lane
London W12 7RJ
Tel: 0181 743 8000

British Association of Journalists
94 Fleet Street
London EC4Y lDE
Tel: 0171 353 3003

British Film Institute
21 Stephen Street
London WlP 2LN
Tel: 0171 255 1444

British Institute of Professional Photography
Anwell End,
Ware. Herts SG12 9HN

Bureau of Freelance Photographers
Focus House
497 Green Lanes
London N13 4BP
Tel: 0181 882 3315

Chartered Institute of Journalists
2 Dock Offices
Surrey Quays Road
London SE16 2XL
Tel: 0171 252 1187

Comedy Writers Association of Great Britain
61 Parry Road, Ashmore Park
Wolverhampton WVll 2PS
Tel: 01902 722 729

Earnley Concourse
Droves Lane
Earnley
Chichester, West Sussex
PO21 21A
Tel: 01243 670392

International Correspondence School
8 Elliot Place,
Clydeway Centre
Glasgow G3 8EF
Scotland
Tel: 0141 221 2926

Irish Writers Union
19 Parhnell Square
Dublin 1
Republic of Ireland
Tel: 00 3531 872 1302

Market Research Bureau
15 Northburgh Street
London EC1V OAH
Tel: 0171 490 4911

Mills and Boon (Publishers) Ltd
Eton House
18-24 Paradise Road
Richmond, Surrey
TW9 1SR
Tel: 0181 948 0444

National Union of Journalists
Acorn House
314 - 320 Grays Inn Road
London WClX 8DP
Tel: 0171 278 7916

New Playwrights Trust
Interchange Studios
Dalby Street
London SW5 3NQ
Tel: 0171 284 2818

Romantic Novelists Association
35 Ruddlesway
Windsor. Berks
SL4 5SF
Tel: 01753 867100

Royal Photographic Society
The Octagon
Milsom Street
Bath BAl lDN

Script City (Film & TV Scripts)
Suite 5134
19 Cheval Place
London SW7 1EW
Tel: 0171 413 9985

Society of Authors
84 Drayton Gardens
London SW10 9SB
Tel: 0171 373 6642

Society of Women's Writers and Journalists
114 Whitehall Road
London E4 6DW
Tel: 0181 529 0886

Theatre Writers Union
c/o G & TU
Central House
Upper Woburn Place
London WlH OHY
Tel: 0181 673 6636

Welsh Union of Writers
Botacho Wyn
Nefyn
Gwynedd, LL53 6HA
Tel: 01758 720430

Writers Guild of Great Britain
430 Edgeware Road
London W2 lEH
Tel: 0171 723 8074

Writers Software Company
Suite 137
2 Old Brompton Road
London SW7 3DQ

Publications

Contacts (Stage and Television)
The Spotlight
7 Leicester Place
London WC2H 7BP
Tel: 0171 437 5881

Freelance Market News
Freelance Press Services
Cumberland House
Lissadel Street
Salford M6 6GG
Tel: 0161 702 8225

Freelance Photographer's Market Handbook
Bureau of Freelance Photographers
BFP Books
497 Green Lanes
London N13 4BP
Tel: 0181 882 3315

Freelance Writing and Photography
Tregaraint House
Zennor
St Ives
Cornwall TR26 3DB
Tel: 01736 797061

How To Write For Television
by William Smethurst
How To Books Ltd
Plymbridge House
Estover Road
Plymouth. Devon PL6 7PZ
Tel: 01752 735251/695745

Magazine Writer's Handbook
by Gordon Wells
Published by Allison and Busby
179 Kings Cross Road
London WC1X 9BZ
Tel: 0171 833 1042

Media Guide
Published by Fourth Estate Ltd
6 Salem Road
London W2 4BU
Tel: 0171 727 8993

1000 Markets For Freelance writers
by Robert Palmer
Published by Judy Piatkus (Publishers) Ltd
5 Windmill Street
London WlP 1HF

35mm Photographer's Handbook
by Julian Calder & John Garrett
Published by Marshall Editions Ltd
170 Piccadilly
London WlV 9DD
Tel: 0171 629 0079

Willings Press Guide
Published by Reed Information Services
Windsor Court
East Grinstead House
East Grinstead RH19 lXA
Tel: 01342 326972

Writers' and Artists' Yearbook
Published by A & C Black (Publishers) Ltd
35 Bedford Row
London WClR 4JH
Tel: 0171 242 0946

Writer's Diary
Available from Know How Publications
Cowieslinn
Eddleston
Peebleshire EH45 8QZ
Scotland

Writing For Radio
by Rosemary Horstmann
Published by A & C Black Ltd
35 Bedford Row
London WC1R 4JH
Tel: 0171 242 0946

The Writer's Handbook
Published by Macmillan Publishers Ltd
25 Eccleston Place
London SW1W 9NF
Tel: 0171 881 8000

Writer's Monthly
29 Turnpike Lane
London N8 OEP
Tel: 0181 342 8879

Writer's News
PO Box 4
Nairn IV12 4HU
Scotland
Tel: 01667 454441

Writing - The Hobby That Pays
by Gordon Wells
Published by EFB Publishers Pte Ltd
162 Bukit Merah Central #043545
Singapore 0315